Burdett Hart

The crown lost and restored

Burdett Hart

The crown lost and restored

ISBN/EAN: 9783337270162

Printed in Europe, USA, Canada, Australia, Japan

Cover: Foto ©Suzi / pixelio.de

More available books at **www.hansebooks.com**

BY

BURDETT HART, D. D.,

Author of "Biblical Epochs," "Studies of the Model Life," "Aspects of
Heaven," "Always Upward"

BOSTON
The Pilgrim Press
CHICAGO
1899

To the Church
of which he was ordained
the Pastor
fifty-three years ago
and of which by whose courtesy he is now
the Pastor Emeritus
this Volume is affectionately inscribed
by the Author.

CONTENTS

THE DISCROWNING OF MAN

"The crown is fallen from our head: Woe unto us! for we have sinned."—*Lamentations* 5 :16.

DELIVERED IN CENTRAL PRESBYTERIAN CHURCH, PHILADELPHIA.

At first man possessed a limited regality. Dominion was given unto him. Nature, throughout its animate tribes, and partly within its inanimate realm, recognized him as its lord. For him the seasons revolved, seed-time and harvest came in their appointed place, the sunshine and the shower bathed the world, and all things were " in excellent order, peace, and beautiful harmony." To him, as to a monarch, the earth, the air and the waters yielded their tribute, and his revenue was royal. With erect form, with noble front, with the port of a prince, he moved in his wide domain, with no one to dispute his title or to deny him homage. God had put the crown upon his head. Man was king!

Then the world was in tranquillity. That was the Golden Age, the fair and happy past, of which the poets sang, whose return is a burden of prophecy. Then the angels descended among men, and the Lord God walked with his peaceful children.

How long this golden period lasted we can only conjecture. We know that the tempter invaded Eden and that sin robbed man of his glory and his joy. The harmony of nature was broken. The peaceful concord was interrupted. Anarchy and confusion and evil prevailed in Paradise. The angels turned mournfully away and spread their wings in retreat, while emissaries of sin prowled in the bowers which they had frequented. God and man were no more in unison. There was terror in the voice of the Father. The crown was fallen from man's head: woe was upon him, for he had sinned. My subject is,—

The Discrowning of Man.

1. We may consider it in respect to bodily excellences. As he came from the hand of his Maker the first man was perfect. All his physical endowments were of prime order. He was erect, muscular, graceful, strong. Dignity and sweetness were combined in the expression of his face, over which rose the dome in which is the seat of the mind. He was capable of work, and found enjoyment in it. Every pulse beat with vigor; every heart-throb was full and sturdy. He was made for life: made to live and to live on in enjoyment and with health.

Had he stood in his original uprightness he would have lived forever in perpetual youth and robust manliness. As it was, it took a long time to reduce the life of man to its present term: the first generations lived for nearly a thousand years, in wanton strength, braving the Almighty in their fierce incontinence, and wasting their powers in lavish lust. There were giants in the earth in those days, men of stalwart frame and impetuous passions, who filled the world with tumult and transgression, grim and gory Goliaths, great in crime, robust witnesses of the fearfulness of the fall.

Sin interrupted the health and broke the vigor of the body. Pain, disease, languor, feebleness, thenceforward were its heritage. Wearing toil and trouble were to be the costly price of success. The curse came upon the body.

What have we seen since? The eye that looked upon the forbidden fruit has been blinded; the hand that plucked that fruit has been palsied; the heart that lusted for it has been riven. The thorn and the thistle have pierced the wounded flesh; the worn laborer has panted and fainted in exhaustion; the tired invalid has tossed in miserable unrest; whole trains and tribes of diseases have invaded the human system, attacking it in all its functions and piercing it through and through with sharp pains; sorrows have broken upon

human hearts as the surges of the sea break upon
its coasts; and death, in terrible throes, has hurled
the soul and body asunder.

Mankind has had a hard experience, even in the
line of physical suffering. Every limb has been
put to torture. Every sensitive nerve has been
made a telegraphic line of pain. The weight of
their woe has bent the frame so that men have
gone bowed like bulrushes. Hospitals have
been crowded with disfigured patients. One of
the learned professions, employing the time and
tact of trained practitioners, is devoted to the
study and relief of bodily ills. The head is
sick; the heart is diseased; the whole man is
covered with wounds. There are pangs at birth;
there are agonies in living; there are throes
in dying.

And this is man who stood forth so royally at
creation, in perfect organism, in noble dignity, in
the glow and glory of wondrous life! Surely the
crown is fallen from his head. Woe unto him
that he has sinned!

One would look far to find a nobler company of
men than are the peers of England. In them is
the blood of long lines of distinguished ancestry.
There are forms and features expressive of cultured
minds. There are men who tower above their fel-
lows not more in physical endowments than in the
graces and accomplishments of a true refinement.

They are nobles. Yet they are not what all men
would have been in bodily excellences if sin had
been unknown. Every proud peer may have the
experience of pain and writhe as a helpless
sufferer.

2. This discrowning respects the dominion over
the world. Man was at first largely its master.
God gave him authority to subdue the earth and
invested him with dominion over every living
thing that moved upon it. The wide creation was
to minister to him and manifold life was to serve
him.

As the experiment did not go forward far, it is
left to our imagination only to picture the progress
and power of this race. Endowed with sovereignty,
man would have controlled the elements and
wrought out a civilization that would have been
sublime.

We wonder now at the works of early times.
We tread with awe the silent streets of a buried
Nineveh; or sail over the sunken shafts and columns and massive blocks which once adorned and
enriched commercial Tyre; or gaze on the Titanic
works of ancient Egypt, whose ruins are magnificent; or admire the later art of Athens and the
glory of old Rome. We cease to wonder at the
achievements of modern science. It has abridged
distance and annihilated time; it has given voice
to the silent rocks; it has measured the limitless

heavens with a span; it has launched upon the
deep a ship capable of conveying a city within its
hulk, which sways with graceful dignity to the
everlasting pulsation of the sea and moves victoriously to its port.

Yet these, and such as these, are the works of
the discrowned man. Now, nature treats him as
a rival, often as an enemy. He is in conflict with
the beasts of the field, which match their strength
and skill with his. He is a rebel and all things
are rebellious against him. He contends with
reptiles and brutes for even a home in the world.
The sun and the storm strive to make him an outcast, parching the earth into deserts or sweeping
away its products as with the strokes of an aven-
ger.

He is no longer the world's ruler. Lisbon
wails from its gaping earthquakes; buried Pompeii
lifts up its smothered cry from beneath the ashes
and lava which have whelmed its gay and guilty
people; Goldau laments for its fair and virtuous
inhabitants buried in a common grave; coral
floors and halls of the sea send up their requiem
for sunken navies and merchantmen; gloomy
jungles are grim with the bleached skeletons of
men torn by beasts; here and there the lightning
and the tornado have left their fearful path; all
showing that the earth is in no mood to acknowl-
edge its subjection.

If man, with these odds against him, has done so much in art, in architecture, in science, in good learning, in affairs, so that imposing monuments everywhere attest his achievements, what might he not have done with his dominion preserved and asserted? Now, ruins, the broken memorials of what has been, are the most decisive proofs of the greatness of the mortal architect.

The crown is fallen from the head, and the earth shares in the woe of man. The whole creation groans and travails in pain together until now. The earth is waiting in patience for its lord, for the time when this lost sovereignty shall be regained.

3. We may trace this discrowning in the realm of mental endowments. At first, not only were these of a noble rank, for man was made but a little lower than the angels, they were also worthily employed. The intellect was clear and strong, the affections were pure and holy, the will was right. The mind was royal. It sat as king on an undisputed throne. It was in perfect harmony with God. It saw things as he saw them. It was in the image of the divine Father. It was loyal, true, free from fault, growing in knowledge and in every excellence. And what a future opened before it! Heights of vision, of power, of blessedness, invited its ascent. So it might have gone on, without a hindrance, without a stain,

nearer to God forever. The growth of a sinless
mind is one of the sublimest things of which we
can conceive. To it come serene and grand
thoughts; in it well up loving and broad
affections; from it proceed pure purposes and
holy activities. All littleness, all meanness, all
low indulgences are forever absent from such a
mind. It takes in the warm sunshine of the
divine favor and all healthful growths spring up
and flourish and mature within it.

But now, what a ruin is there! I do not speak
of those minds merely in which the reason is
dethroned, of lunatics who gibber and mumble in
cells and in the wards of hospitals, of idiots
whose vacant stare tells of the emptiness within.
But I speak of all minds that have swung loose
from obligation, of the race in its sinfulness which
is the mother of disorder and derangement.

Anarchy and revolt have taken the place of
peace and loyalty. The crown is fallen, and
rebellion riots in the palace of the mind. Woe
unto us that we have sinned! All is downward, not
toward the earth alone, but toward the deeper
depths, toward the deep damnation of perdition, the
fathomless abyss of despair. This is the vandal work
of sin. The metropolis of thought, to which came
up the loaded caravans from distant regions of wealth
and productiveness; to which thronged ships
from ports across restless seas, laden with the

spoils of warriors and with the products of labor, to which journeyed men of learning, great artists and pious priests, ambassadors of empires and princes of the blood, has been sacked and polluted by the hosts of sin, its cathedrals have been burned with fire and its palaces leveled to the dust.

The world of matter, in all its gloomy desolations, in the sack of temples and the overthrow of cities, presents nothing so dreadful as the ruins of mind. The genius of history weeps at the loss of the Alexandrian library, by which the gathered trophies of ancient learning were swept into oblivion in a day; but a single mind, thrown from its orbit and projected into the whirl and darkness of sin, is a far sadder loss. We lament the destruction of the choice works of ancient art, whose broken fragments, rescued from the wave and the rubbish, are the admiration of all students, in which might have been given to us the form and features of the men who made history, but far more lamentable is the waste and the perdition of the souls that were gifted, souls that might have been great in achievement and immortal in goodness.

The downfall of a man is more than the downfall of an empire. The latter can be repaired and a nobler empire take its place made wise by the ruin of the former; but there is no repair or recovery of a soul that is lost forevermore.

2

scepter passed from his hands; so the woe of depravity enshrouded him in its gloom and wretchedness. It is pitiful to see such downfall.

About a century ago there was one who rose from a humble rank with imperial strides to the throne of the most warlike and gallant of the nations. Power came spontaneously to his hands. His victorious legions were successful on all battle-fields and against all armies. He gave away crowns with royal generosity. He brought to his gorgeous capital the treasures of conquered lands, and enriched his palaces with the chief works of art. The enthusiasm of his people for their hero rose beyond all precedent. The humblest conscript was devoted to his fortunes. At times it seemed as though he were to realize the wild dream of universal empire. Formidable combinations against him dissolved at the magic of his sword. His name thrilled through continents.

From that he fell. Almost alone, on a barren rock, dashed on every side by the billows, he was doomed to weary years of exile; and there he fretted his great life away, watched by the sleepless eye of his enemy, and forgotten by the friends who had shared his successful fortunes. It was force alone that made that emperor yield up his crown.

More than three centuries ago, a monarch, in

the midst of life, with crowns and coronets on his head and in his hands, laid down his royalty and stepped from an imperial throne into the retirement of a secluded monastery. He was born to the throne, and before he was of age he wore the regal mantle. On many battle-fields he proved himself the foremost warrior of the time, and his kingdom widened and grew upon his hands until the sun went not down upon his realm. For forty years he had accustomed himself to the exercise of power, until the atmosphere of the court and the camp was necessary to his life. Yet he left it all, and with pale face passed his scepter to another. In his soul he felt himself unequal to his burdens. His day of triumph had passed and quick reverses were dashing his dreams. He fled to the shadows of the mountains and the dull society of monks from fear of calamity that was hounding him.

More than fifteen centuries since one of the ablest emperors of Rome abdicated the throne and retired to his palace by the seashore, where, amidst his extensive and productive gardens, he found repose, and cherished no regret.

But there has been no discrowning like the first. All others have only changed the externals of the parties concerned; the men have remained the same. But this changed both what was external and what was internal as well. It overthrew the

the midst of life, with crowns and coronets on his
head and in his hands, laid down his royalty and
stepped from an imperial throne into the retirement of a secluded monastery. He was born to
the throne, and before he was of age he wore the
regal mantle. On many battle-fields he proved
himself the foremost warrior of the time, and his
kingdom widened and grew upon his hands until
the sun went not down upon his realm. For forty
years he had accustomed himself to the exercise
of power, until the atmosphere of the court and
the camp was necessary to his life. Yet he left
it all, and with pale face passed his scepter to
another. In his soul he felt himself unequal to
his burdens. His day of triumph had passed and
quick reverses were dashing his dreams. He fled
to the shadows of the mountains and the dull
society of monks from fear of calamity that was
hounding him.

More than fifteen centuries since one of the
ablest emperors of Rome abdicated the throne
and retired to his palace by the seashore, where,
amidst his extensive and productive gardens, he
found repose, and cherished no regret.

But there has been no discrowning like the first.
All others have only changed the externals of the
parties concerned; the men have remained the
same. But this changed both what was external
and what was internal as well. It overthrew the

II

THE CHRISTIAN'S CORONATION

" Henceforth there is laid up for me the crown of righteousness, which the Lord, the righteous judge, shall give to
me at that day : and not only to me, but also to all them that
have loved his appearing."— 2 *Timothy* 4 : 8.

———

At Calvary Church, Philadelphia.

of Rome that he projected his great work of the
Decline and Fall.   There was a magic in those
silent and dreary emblems which summoned before
him the scenes and persons of the past.   He saw
the forum once vocal with Roman eloquence,
the temples once hallowed with Roman worship,
the coliseum once crowded with Roman spec-
tators, and the streets and the dwellings once full
of Roman life, springing into reality.   Again the
senate sat and the voices of Rome's great orators
were heard.   Again the conquering legions poured
along the broad highways, returning from victories to their triumphal welcome home.   Again the
old men and women, the young men and maidens,
mingled in the festivals and filled the city with the
tides of life.   Again uprose stately column and
capital, and walls that had long been prostrate,
adorned anew by architects and crowded with the
noble statuary of artists.   He had only to follow
the suggestions of what he saw lying grandly and
gloomily around him to rebuild and people the
seven-hilled city and to live back its historic life.

So as we look on the moral ruins of the race,
on powers prostrate and perverted, on souls hurled
from their places of light and beauty, on minds
deranged and chained to earth that might have
trooped upward like angels to the throne, on a
dominion that is lost, on forms torn and suffering
and bent under the burden of sin, on clashing

interests and passions all at war, on the turmoil
and woe of men, we feel the shock of the fall
and the scroll of a dark history unrolls before us.
There is an aspect of the ruin of what was once
great and good. The crown is fallen from a regal
head; woe is unto us that we have sinned!

United with this, separable from it, though
mingled with it like the warp and woof of a fabric,
is the aspect of restoration.

The view of the world is not all dark. Light
beams amidst the shadows. There are tones of
pure melody thrilling through the discords. As
in old Oriental ruins, amidst heaps of rubbish,
there will now and then flash out the light of a
precious stone telling of the wealth and nobility
that once were there, so with all that is dark
in our discrowned humanity, we may see some
brightness, the relic of our earliest past, the
prophecy of our brighter future. The costly gems
of the crown, flung loosely in its fall, can be
regained and wrought into a more regal coronet.
The Scriptures are full of the prophecy of a
restoration. They tell us, in varied speech, of a
crown that is to be worn by redeemed man. The
old royalty is to be regained. The lost dominion
is to be acquired again. The prince who has
been outlawed, who has been driven far from his
ancestral towers and whose enemies have hunted
him from land to land, is to return welcomed by

been and others had risen in a corresponding
ratio. The throne within him was more than the
throne without.

And such is the change wrought by religion.
It infuses royal ideas into the mind. It gives its
possessor self-control and the dignity of noble
character.

The greatest king is he who has the sublime
mastery of himself. The monarch of millions may
be less royal than many of his subjects. It is not
titles, nor crown jewels, nor the purple robe, can
give to any one true kingship. There is a higher
coronation. It is the enthronement of the man's
own self: so that he is no longer as a slave, so
that he no longer wears a yoke of subjection to
any low indulgence or passion, so that pure and
worthy motives meet response within him, so that
he is brought into the company and communion
of regal souls to whom belongs the kinghood of
the ages. Such a man is a crowned monarch.
No visible hand may have placed upon his brow
the gemmed coronet. From no consecrated person may he have received the benediction that is
accorded to kings. Through no line of royal
ancestors may have descended to him the scepter
that he is to wield. No plaudits of admiring multitudes may have announced his coronation. But
he walks the world every inch a king. He has
met himself and conquered, and there is thence-

forth no other foe so formidable. He who is master of himself is master of all others. There is no
force can subdue him who is victor of himself.
The greatest empire is that whose imperial boundaries are the man's own circumference. There are
no territorial lines that can include and confine the
measure of a single soul.

The greatest emperor may be baser than the
lowest serf within his realm. Some humble serf
may rank him in the heraldry of princes. It is
not outward pomp and rank can ennoble mind.
Royalty is within; its banners are good and holy
works. The emperor may be base in mind, held
in thraldom by imperious passions and degrading
habits; the serf may be noble in thought and feeling and free purpose, in all but the mere outward
place and pomp. Who would not prefer the
crown of the latter to that of the former?

The king in Christ Jesus has self-dominion.
Once he was a slave. Now he has prison cells for
the traitors who rise up within the palace of his
own mind, and they are thrust down there and
held there.

He who can walk the world in this freedom is
the anointed one, is king by divine right. He
dwells in a palace built by no human hand; his
courtiers are high thoughts and pure motives; his
executive is the loyal and unconquerable will.
This is royalty; not that which rests on the huz-

zas of a fickle populace, but on the election of a
soul that God has made immortal.

2. The Christian is crowned by virtue of his
regal possessions. He has no limited empire,
with the territories of rivals and enemies bordering
his own who may invade and enslave him. Some
great conquerors have been fascinated by the
dream of universal empire. How vain the dream!
One such died after a debauch, lamenting that he
could gain no more; another fell by the daggers
of assassins; another met his solitary fate on a
barren rock in mid-sea.

Religion realizes this ideal. The possession of
the world is restored in Christ. And not this
alone, but all worlds become the inheritance of the
saints. Says the apostle, "All things are yours;
whether Paul, or Apollos, or Cephas, or the world,
or life, or death, or things present, or things to
come; all are yours."

We gain more in Christ than we lost in Adam.
We lost one world; we gain the universe. We
lost one crown; we gain another far more brilliant.
We receive tribute from all worlds. The past,
with its wealth of experience, with its history of
martyrs and its bold testimony of prophets and
confessors, with its revolutions, its sufferings, its
science, its psalms and hymns, the soul-gushings
of heroes and of seers, is all for us. For us the
world stands, loaded with its immortal freight, yet

burning with pent-up fires that flame and roar for outlet.

For the Christian is to be the future, bright with promise, holy with its universal love. He is to sit with Christ on his throne; a joint-heir with the divine Son to the kingdom that has no limits. His empire is universal. Such regal possessions dwarf the kingdoms and estates of this world.

3. This coronation admits to royal society. In common opinion, there is a divinity that hedges round a king. Royal blood is considered as rather better blood than that which runs in ordinary veins. It certainly has been more bloody. Regal families dwell apart. Few can gain access to them. The old hereditary monarchs carry a disdainful air and tone toward those who have risen from the vulgar level to thrones. Cromwell was stigmatized as a parvenu, and so were the Napoleons. Nothing but their power unbarred for them the palaces of their neighbors. When Cromwell was dead, his body was dug up and hung; when he was living, his imperial arms brought pliant ambassadors to his court from most powerful states. The Napoleons had conferences and visits with monarchs who would have frowned them out of their presence if they had dared.

The new birth of the soul makes one a hereditary king. His heraldry is most regal. His ancestry is divine. His fraternity is that of right royal souls. The loftiest and purest society is freely open to him. The really great of this world are his best friends, and they invite his presence with fraternal affection. The kings in thought, in purpose, in holy achievement, the foremost men in learning, in benevolence, in charity, whose names are more enduring than brass, or the marble that commemorates royal deeds, the saints of all ages, laureled poets, ordained priests, crowned princes, these are his peers. He has daily audience, too, with the King of kings, not with the dread of the suppliant of old, not with the sense of remoteness and coldness, but as a son with a father, as a friend with a friend. He is a son of God. The royalty of heaven is his.

4. There is the enthronement of God in the renewed man. Sin, while it banished man from paradise, banished God also from man. He was shut out from the human soul, and that wonderful organism, which had been illumined with divine light, became dark. Man was alone in his rebellion; he was, in most suggestive phrase, without God. But the restoration by Christ brings God back again. It unites the soul and its Maker. It places the king on his rightful throne. God and man are at one. Here is the true regality.

Man is not himself when he is separated from the Godhead. His powers work normally only

when they work in the divine will. Their action
is earthly when man lives apart; it is heavenly
when he lives in God, and when God lives in him.
There should be but one supreme will in all the
universe. All other wills should glide into that
and work in unison with it. It belongs to us, as
the highest law of our life, the disregard of which
leaves us dead, to know no will but God's. Our
life should come from him. We should, as a per-
manent, all-controlling decision of the whole mind,
elect God as our all, in whom and for whom we
are to live. That endows us with a divine life.
Our sustenance is from God, and the whole movement of our being is in perfect harmony with his.
More and more he takes possession of us, living
out his pure agency through us.

So God is enthroned in the Christian. He
lives, because God lives in him; he reigns, because God reigns in him. He thus sits down with
Christ on his throne; he is one with the world's
King, and his coronation is divine. To such kinghood does the restoration exalt the renewed be-
liever. And, as the sovereignty of Christ is real-
ized most fully in heaven, it is there that the final
and perfect coronation of the Christian is to be
witnessed. Here he is a king in disguise. But
he is to be recognized and crowned hereafter. He
is to come like a conqueror to Zion. An eternal
weight of glory is to be given to him. I appoint

unto you, said our Lord, a kingdom as my father
hath appointed unto me; that ye may sit on
thrónes. When the son of man shall sit on the
throne of his glory, ye also shall sit upon thrones.
If children, then heirs; heirs of God and joint-
heirs with Christ. The praises of that world shall
be given, as the Revelation tells us, unto Him
that loved us and hath made us kings and priests,
unto God and his Father.

There have been many majestic assemblages,
when the crowns of ancient kingdoms and empires
have been placed upon anointed and consecrated
heads. Nobles of the realm, the venerable digni-
taries of the state and of the Church, ambassadors
of foreign powers, great scholars, the beauty of
peerless women, the pomp of military pageantry,
and the charm of music, have united to give splendor and glory to the event. But earth has witnessed nothing so imposing and beautiful as the
coronations of heaven. Its inhabitants are the
elect of earth, the élite of all lands and ages, the
loyal and holy angels of God. Amongst these,
in the midst of such august and holy assemblages,
are the sons of God to receive the investiture of
their undecaying crowns.

There have been restorations in secular history.
Five centuries and a half before the Christian era,
after a captivity of seventy years, the conqueror of
Babylon sent forth a herald throughout his realms

to proclaim a return of all the people of the God
of heaven to their own land. From Babylon and
from other cities of the East, in great caravans,
the Hebrew exiles, with their camels and horses
and beasts of burden, took up their march for the
sacred hills of Palestine. For four months they
traveled on, and then, with psalms and cymbals
and exulting shouts, they ascended the summits of
Jerusalem, and reared an altar to the living God,
amidst the ruins of the ancient temple. Joyful was
that restoration of the Hebrews to their estates and
worship.

Two hundred years ago a proud pageant was
enacted in old England. On the white beach of
Dover, amidst the acclaim of the immense multitude who thronged to receive him, landed the
exiled king of England. For years he had been a
stranger to his throne and an outlaw from his
realm. But the people had called back their
monarch. Nobles who had remained loyal,
scarred soldiers who had followed the standards
of the Protector, statesmen and people, vied to do
him honor. Banners waved. Cannon thundered
forth their welcome. Bells rang out the joy of
the nation. Songs, flowers, shouts, tears, expressed the popular heart. All the way from the
sea to the capital the road was hedged with
masses of the people, all wearing a look of gladness. London was alive with joy. The king

entered that old city like a conqueror, in triumph. Old men had never seen such a tide of enthusiasm. The streets, every window and balcony, the spires of churches and the roofs of houses, teemed with loyal men and happy women. The intoxication of gladness and gratitude was contagious and universal. Never did crowned king receive a more spontaneous and popular ovation. This event is known in history as the Restoration.

Forty-five years ago an analogous scene was witnessed in the rival nation across the channel. Bursting from his exile at Elba the discrowned emperor landed on the shore of France. The mountaineers of Dauphiné hailed his return. His old soldiers, sent out to apprehend him, rushed from their ranks, prostrated themselves at his feet, and with mingled tears and shouts welcomed him as their emperor. Resistance was in vain. The great marshals of the empire ranked themselves in his favor, and the army, wild with enthusiasm, joined their fortunes to those of the greatest soldier of the age. With characteristic impetuosity he flew on to Paris, where he was received with unbounded manifestations of exultation. Crowds of officers and soldiers filled the palace court, on whose uplifted arms he was borne within the historic walls of the Tuileries, where beauty and bravery joined in greeting his arrival. Again the emperor wore the diadem of France.

Feebly can these scenes, and such as these, in history, represent to us the restoration of the soul and its final coronation. They were scenes of a day, swept from sight with the swift progress of events.

But the blessed crown of the Christian is enduring. It will shine when the jewels of all human coronets have paled and turned to dust. It will grow more brilliant and more precious as eternity moves on.

We are not, then, to turn despondingly back to the glory that we have lost and to pine for the shattered crown of our first father; rather we are diligently to win that crown of righteousness which the Lord will give unto all those who love his appearing.

III

THE ENDLESSNESS OF CHRIST'S LOVE

Having loved his own which were in the world, he loved them unto the end.—*John* 13 : 1.

———

AT INSTALLATION IN CONGREGATIONAL CHURCH, VINE-LAND, N. J., Sept., 1872,

THE ENDLESSNESS OF CHRIST'S LOVE

The love that endures is most worthy, is, in fact, the only love that is worth having. The affection that gushes like a geyser, steaming away in hot spurts and shooting upward with imposing effect for twenty minutes, is of no practical account and is not really anything great as an exhibition. Friendship is a principle as well as a passion. It is based on character. It is built up like a wall of granite, of shapely blocks, squarely matched, to stand through storms, through changes, through convulsions. Time does not destroy it, but only gives it solidity. Other principles or passions do not supplant it; amidst them it endures, retaining its early characteristics.

Just here we might distinguish the true friendship from its counterfeit. The semblance is weak and transient and easily ended; the true abides, holding its own as the years pass and the revolutions occur and the orbits of human thought

change.   A selfish love ends with the occasion
that excited it.   A true love waxes stronger in
trial and survives misfortune and remains when
other things are lost.   I have said, *a selfish love*,
I should have said, a selfish passion; for *love* is
unselfish; it sacrifices for its object; it remits its
own choices and pleasures for another's welfare
and gratification; it finds its purest delight in the
happiness of the loved one.   That friendship
which is exacting and selfish is short-lived, as it
ought to be.   The friendship that is generous and
sacrificial is enduring and noble.   In that sweetest story of Hebrew friendship, the monarch's
son, the regal heir of the kingdom, puts even the
crown upon the head of his friend.   Love could
feel no loss.   In touching elegy, at his early dying,
his fortunate friend memorized his wonderful
affection: " Thy love to me was wonderful, passing the love of women."   And in the renowned
story of Grecian friendship, death was not too
strong a test; the utter willingness of one to die
for the other broke the tyrant's heart.   Love
could do what power could not do.

The real friendship lasts; it lasts up to the line
that divides the seen from the unseen; it lasts
beyond, into the unseen, but real; in the realm of
widest thought and purest affection, where
acquaintance is brotherhood and union is eternal.
We have felt its thrill hard on the confines of

heaven, as we have gone close to mysteries with
those who were leaving us, as hands have
unclasped ours to take hold of the hands of
angels. The love of the lifetime, grown strong in
the experiences which have been shared together,
hallowed by trial, gladdened by common joys,
has been fullest and ripest as the earth-life has
ended, has glowed with warmest tenderness and
devotion amidst the sinking of the bodily and
mental faculties, as the greatest glory of the day
gathers in crimson and golden flames around the
sinking sun. We cannot doubt its continuance
beyond, where our eyesight does not reach, but
where our soul-sight pierces, in realms that are
real though unknown, peopled by those who were
with us, and are still of us, our kindred by closest
relationship, one with us by common, sacred
blood, and with whom we soon shall be. For the
friendship that endures rests in the common love
to Christ. All else ends. The friendship in noble
pursuits, as in the researches of science, in the
lore of letters, in the problems of statecraft, in
whatever is essentially of the earth, must become
only a memory when the earth and the works of
it shall be burned up. But the love that is in
Christ centers in him and endures with him and is
eternal. It has the qualities of his love. "As I
have loved you, that ye also love one another."
"That the love wherewith thou hast loved me

may be in them, and I in them." Christ's love
lasted. It survived his fortunes and their fortunes,
all that was propitious, all that was untoward, the
hail to kingship, the hurrying to crucifixion, their
following, their flight. Through all it beamed on,
as steadily as the light of a fixed star. " Having
loved his own who were in the world, he loved
them unto the end." My subject is :

The Endlessness of Christ's Love.

In his tender and affectionate references to his
Father he often made mention of the wonderful
love that subsisted between them. He speaks in
comparison, " As the Father hath loved me."
And he would live and act, " That the world may
know that I love the Father." As though his purest happiness were there he says, " I . . . abide in
his love." And through all the woe of his earthly
life, remained the untold comfort that he should
" go to the Father." In the solitariness of his
work he was not alone, " because the Father is
with me." In the absorbing earnestness of his
remarkable prayer for his disciples, in which he
moves the paternal heart in their behalf by the
urgency of their common love, he says, " For thou
lovedst me before the foundation of the world."

This expression carries the thought back into
the eternity that was, before the creations began.
Then, in all the countless ages, when the blessed,

infinite Persons of the Godhead were alone, in the glory and perfections of their being, they found the purest happiness in their own society and love. Not a world had rolled out into space, not a creature had been formed and informed with life. Only God was. The universe was full of him alone. Throughout the eternal past, in unbroken, countless milleniums, back beyond all thought of duration the Father and the Son had lived and loved together. For their own happiness the Persons of the Godhead needed no creation. In the stillness of the unpeopled space, in the solitariness of their sole being, they were infinitely happy in each other. They were more to each other than all other beings could be to them, though stars should be flung forth through the boundless void and every star be crowded with populations. In that endless past Christ was the dearly beloved of the Father; and the Father was all in all to him. He defines his own place there as " in the bosom of the Father." Phrase full of suggestion! Here is nearness and dearness, oneness of heart, perfectness of love. And so they loved unto the beginning. Christ was used to a persistent love. He had loved long and with unchanging steadfastness before he loved his own which were in the world.

We cannot, by any experiences of ours, measure the infinite love of these divine Persons; but perfect and precious as it was, it did not stand in the

4

way of the Redeemer's work for man.   That work
was not hastily decided upon.   It belonged to
the counsels of eternity.   It entered into the whole
plan of the world's creating and populating.   The
Redemption runs back in the thought and purpose
of God to the remotest past.   He who made the
world would save the world.   There was an ante-
advent love.   Christ's coming was only the fulfillment of his eternal purpose.

There was a long time of waiting and of watching.   Not only through those milleniums which
slowly passed after sin began its work of desolation, but through countless durations before that,
was the Lord intent on salvation.   When the fullness of the time should come, he would be ready
to be offered.   He ever looked forward to his
redemptive undertaking as certain to come.
Understanding all that was involved in it, he
would enter upon and finish it.   Love was the
underlying principle of redemption.   " For God
so loved the world, that he gave his only begotten
Son."   And "the love of Christ, which passeth
knowledge" moved him to come into the world.
From eternity he had thought of his own; all his
other vast plans involved this, that he should die
for them; their redemption, by his own offering,
was as certain as the future.   It was, then, no new
thing, no suddenly devised interposition to stop
the woe of sin.   It was old.   It was older than

creation.   It runs back of all our numeration.   Its
origin is in the remote eternity.   It was a divine,
eternal purpose.   When brought, therefore, to
actual experience it would stand.   Having loved
his own which were in the world, he would love
them unto the end.   He would not abandon them.
He would not permit his greatest undertaking to
come to nought.   It was an eternal purpose which
would move on to the end.

At last the waiting time was over; on the world
was the advent of its Creator to save it.   He came
to fulfil the promises which had rolled forth in
prophetic utterances; to fulfil his own divine plan
of human rescue.   The devotion with which he
gave himself for his own assured the endlessness
of his love for them.   All else gave way to that.
All those things that are attractive to all other
minds he put away, he did not even stop to consider.   Power, wealth, learning, influence, success,
as men look at them, were not within the scope
of his life.   He moved along another plane.   He
held steadily before him another object.   These
things of the world did not belong to him.   He
had left heaven on a different errand.   He had
appeared on the earth as its divine Redeemer.   Sin
was doing its tragic work and leaving everywhere
its terrible tracks.   It was spoiling human love.   It
was hurling the finest minds into wretchedness and
ruin.   It was laying its withering touch on the

noblest works of men. It was making the world one vast charnel-house, filled with graves and piled with dead.

And Christ came as its Deliverer, leaving heaven and its glory behind and assuming all the burdens and sorrows and sufferings that were necessary in the fulfillment of his mission. He gave himself to this one work. He was tempted to abandon it, but temptation had no power over him. He was rejected by those whom he came to save, but their cruel rejection did not turn him aside. He was led forth as a lamb to the slaughter, but he bore his own cross to the place of crucifixion.

At one time, marvel of marvels! the Father forsook him, but he trod the wine-press alone. On, from the beginning to the fearful end, through all obstacles, against all enemies, under all heavy burdens, amidst scorn and sorrow and unutterable anguish at times, he pressed with a fortitude that did not falter and an affection that was infinite. Every place where he toiled and taught became a memorial of his devotion. He lifted Nazareth from its ignoble obscurity to the foremost rank in the thought of the world. Bethlehem gained a greater glory from its association with his name than from its historic fame as a royal city. He invested Samaria with peculiar honor as the Teacher and the Saviour of its despised population.

Capernaum thrills our hearts with its voices of
bane and of blessing, with its works of mercy and its
utterances of woe, from the same divine Person,
who would wish to save, but who could not fail to
forewarn of the evil that was sure to come. Tabor
and Olivet and Bethany received a new sacredness
from his association with them. Every path on
which he traveled through Judæa and Gallilee was
thenceforward a sacred way, on which the feet of
pilgrims from all lands tread with reverence. The
waves of Tiberias and the waters of the Jordan roll
evermore as in unceasing anthem to his praise.
Jerusalem, city of God, joy of the whole earth, is
consecrated more by his tears and precious words,
by his benedictions and his agonies, than by the
coronations of its kings and the royalties of its
thrones and the sacredness of its priesthood and
its temples. In every place, in all conditions, one
solemn purpose controlled him. His whole life
was given for man. The soreness of his own lot
did not make him swerve; no more did the weakness and waywardness of his chosen disciples. He
put up with denial, he endured betrayal, he went
straight on to crucifixion. Calvary became consecrate in the sacred thought and feeling of the
world, and the cross, on which the Redeemer died,
became the holy emblem of all that is most precious to men. He loved unto death. He commended his love for us in that, while we were yet

sinners, he died for us. Such love as this can
know no end.

Furthermore, the achievements of his love—
what we have already seen of it— are prophetic of
the future union in love of Christ and his own,
through a coming eternity. Having loved as he
has in this world, he will love in the coming world.
Having loved in mortality, he will love in immortality. Having loved in weakness, he will love in
power. Having loved in dishonor, he will love
in glory. Having loved in the bodily life, he will
love in the spiritual life.

He will greet his own on "the other side."
Whatever their earthly homes may have been,
however obscure and humble, he will open to them
"mansions" there. Some from the toil of slaves,
some from the wretchedness of poverty, all from
the risks and uncertainties of the earthly service,
he will raise to thrones. It is his imperial purpose that they shall be with him where he is, that
they may behold his glory, that they may share
his kingship, that they may unceasingly enjoy his
love. Honors and positions here are subject to
inevitable reverses. The favorite of to-day may be
the outlaw of to-morrow. But the positions of
heaven, once gained, are never lost. The crowns
of that world are subject to no corrosion. The
friendship of Christ is eternal. He will love to the
end. The measureless progression of unbounded

futurities will reach no limit and no diminution of his infinite affection. It will grow by its own use and gratification.

As the multiplication of a single planted grain, increasing year by year, in geometrical ratio, will at length cover a continent with its opulent harvests, so the love of Christ will fill all the eternities with its abounding fullness and make all loyal and loving hearts infinitely and forever glad in their blessed union to him. We know little of the occupations and the prerogatives of the heavenly life; but as Christ's work has made this world blessed and given sweetness to service here and inspired human hearts with song and affluent hope and every grace that is divine, so will it make heaven a happy world to all the saved, and give inspiration to every service and every song and every sentiment forever and ever. He who loved to the end here will love his own with an endless affection in that world that shall know no end.

This established doctrine of the endlessness of Christ's love is full of the most suggestive encouragements to us. He loves his own, but not those only. He loves all, and he died for all because he loved them. Between himself and his own is a personal friendship, growing out of the very fact of their acceptance of him and of their union to him. It is the dearest of all relationships. It overpasses the sacred attachments of kindred; the

love that unites us in our precious homes to our
other selves, to parent, to child, to brother. We
cannot measure this love for those with whom we
stand for weal or woe, in life or death, for those
who have given us birth and for us would give
themselves, for the children whose grand immortalities are lodged within our influence, for those
with whom we have grown in stature and in learning and in the world's ways. But in the test times
even this gives way to the unspeakable love for the
dear Redeemer who ranks immeasurably all other
friends. We must put him foremost. The martyrs, dying in scourgings and in flames and in the
loss of all things, have spoken the watchword for
the centuries, "Christ only." And if those who
are not now his own would come to him, in full
acceptance of his sincere invitation, they, too, might
be embraced in his endless love.

But for those who are his, this truth already is
full of blessed suggestion and assurance. Accepting, fully believing in our hearts, this divine fact of
the endlessness of the Redeemer's love, we should
recognize the proof of it *in the joys and abounding blessings of our lives.* The springs, mingled in
the secret and subtle alchemy of nature, whose clear
waters flow in unfailing streams for the health and
invigoration of our bodies, are the gift of the Father
of all to his tired and worn children. And all our
springs of happiness are in Him who is the life of

our souls. The world is bright because Christ is the light of it. He dwells with us, and so our homes are full of content and love. He walks with us, and, therefore, the way is pleasant. He fills our hearts with happiness, and so the songs that burst from them are songs of gladness. It is right to recognize Christ in all his relations to us. Our blessings do not come in the course of nature, in the ordering of prudence, as the gift of friends, so much as they come from Christ. Back of nature and prudence and friendship is Christ. He works in all these for his own. So we should not put the less foremost, but always the greater. The distinction between the Christian and the sinner has been thus expressed: one is grateful for the good received, the other is glad. One discerns Christ and his heart goes out in bounding gratitude to him. The other receives his blessings as coming in the ordinary course of things and his heart is full of gladness. Those lives of saints have been most beaming that have been inspired by this recognition of Christ. They have discerned him whom they have not seen. They have taken every blessing as from the outstretched hand of a visible Saviour. The crowning sweetness of every cup of joy has been that he gave it.

Embracing the truth before us in all its richness and fullness, we should *accept the painful discipline of our life* as given us also by his love. Religion does not exempt from trial. It sometimes seems as though the best had the hardest earthly lot. Certainly the followers of Christ are in tutelage for a higher life. And this involves, possibly necessitates, painful discipline. Were this world all brightness and joyousness, they might lose heaven, might at least lose that place in heaven for which the Master qualifies his own. Whatever comes in this needful trial, comes from him who loves them unto the end. They may endure hardship, prolonged, wearing, nothing going well with them, their plans failing, their hopes turning into ashes and all their way being one of disappointment. This is extreme. But we have seen such saints. Very often it comes to pass that they suffer the loss of earthly treasure. By unforeseen calamity, as by fire or flood or the failure of others, the accumulations of years are swept away. Having lived in comfort or in luxury, they are reduced to poverty. Or sickness comes, laying them aside from service, taking them from the ways of business and pleasure and usefulness, and confining them to the four walls of a secluded room, where comparatively alone they must bear the trial. Or, in still heavier affliction, they lose dearest friends, for whom they have lived, for whom they could die, whose being was so enwrapped with their own

that in the loss all the fibers and textures of their
life are torn apart. Under all this experience,
they know that they are his own and that he
loves them unto the end, and with this assurance
they accept his chastening.   Said one, " I love
the rod.   How gentle are the strokes I receive !
How severe those I deserve ! "   And one of old,
" Though he slay me, yet will I wait for him."

The full acceptance of this truth conducts us
readily, possibly without our cognizance, *to the
rest of faith*, for which the earnest Christian soul
seeks.   Let the fact possess us in its superlative
meaning that Christ loves us, loves us always,
loves us to the end, and we shall take him at
his word; we shall ask him for blessings, as our
children ask us, stretching forth the hand to
receive even while we ask, expecting the answer
while yet we call. We shall trust him at all
times, especially in times of straitness and darkness, especially when human help fails. We shall
trust him fully, for ourselves, for others, for the
present, for the future as well, and so for time and
for eternity.   Such love admits this.   Such love
requires this.   Christ's endless love constrains us
to an endless assurance of faith. We shall ask
because we believe.   And we shall believe that
we receive because we ask him.

Finally, this truth becoming regnant in our
hearts would make us *conquerors in the last*

struggle.   There is no thought that has such
overcoming power in death as the thought of
the love of Christ.   Even to the faint-hearted, to
those who have through their lifetime been subject to bondage, whose pleasant pathway has
been shadowed by the dread of the dark valley,
there have come courage and freedom and light
as the Saviour has graciously revealed himself to
them in the dying hour.   He is with his own
when they need him most.   His strength is for
their weakness.   He will never, never, never
leave them.   Precious in the sight of the Lord
is the death of his saints.   The last words that
Luther ever wrote, the day before he died, were,
" Verily I say unto you, if a man keep my saying, he shall never taste of death."   And an
hour before his death he prayed, " O my heavenly
Father, I thank thee that thou hast revealed in
me thy dear Son Jesus Christ, on whom I believe,
whom I have preached and confessed, whom I
have loved and praised."   And his last words
were, " Thou hast redeemed me, O God of truth."
And when his dearest friend, the gentle Melanc-
thon, followed him, the glory of heaven bright-
ened around him and to a friend who asked him,
" Will you have anything else ? " he joyfully
answered, " Nothing else but heaven ! "

A member of our church who lately died was
asked by her husband, " Do you know who are

here with you?" And her answer was, "I know that Jesus is here." Her eyes, dimmed to mortal sight, discerned the loving Lord.

A frail maiden received sudden tidings that her betrothed had been swept by a rushing river beyond the stream of time. She bowed like a bruised reed under the blow too big for tears. Then she lifted her head and said, "My flesh and my heart faileth: but God is the strength of my heart and my portion for ever."

We, my friends, shall not be long apart—they who have gone on before, we who linger a little longer—we shall all, if we are Christ's, parents, children, friends, gather in one delighted company unto our glorious and beloved Saviour. "Who shall separate us from the love of Christ? . . . For I am persuaded, that neither death, nor life, nor angels, nor principalities, nor things present, nor things to come, nor powers, nor height, nor depth, nor any other creature, shall be able to separate us from the love of God, which is in Christ Jesus our Lord."

IV

CONDITIONS OF BELIEF

"If I say truth, why do ye not believe me?"—*John* 8 : 46.

———

At Grand Avenue Church, New Haven.

We have fallen on an era of theological disorder. The old doctrines out of which sturdy character grew are getting roughly handled. The foundations on which the fathers securely builded are reported as weakening and likely to come to disintegration. Those fundamental truths even which have long had evangelical currency, such as the authority of Scripture, the vicariousness of atonement, the eternity of retribution, are not only questioned, but are rejected, as belonging to systems that are effete.

The progress of scientific discovery and the immature claims which it has developed have acted on theological thought to its unrest and have awakened a kind of rival sympathy in this different sphere. It would be unfortunate if, after the vagaries of uncertain science shall have kindly given way to theories which are founded on accepted facts, it should be discovered, that, in the unnecessary ferment, Christianity only had permanently suffered in the loss of some of its greatest principles. Transition periods are rela-

5

tively brief. Truth remains unchanged, whether affirmed or denied. We need to hold to it while the problems of the age are coming to lasting solution; and to hold to it all the more firmly when anchors that had moored us are dragging.

The disorder of faith is not merely affecting those who are leading along the lines of discovery, but it is working among the mass of followers and its disasters are seen in practical, every-day life. It is hard to hold men to the faith as it is set forth in the teachings of Scripture. Proofs, evidences, various and multiplied, on subjects vital to the soul, are not accepted. The plain doctrines of the gospel, the fearful truths of revelation are rejected, and statements, more satisfactory to unrenewed nature, more easy of belief because more harmonious with the feelings, are held and boldly professed. It is not merely that in some quarters there are claims of new revelations as of equal authority with the old Bible, pretended revelations to those whose life and influence convict them as impostors; but we have now to meet the rejection of Holy Scripture by those who have nothing to substitute for it and who glory in their agnosticism; and still further we are confronted by those who, nominally accepting the Scripture, give its declarations no practical credence as they go about to find an easier creed and another way of salvation—or of perdition.

In this debauchment of faith, that we may not let go thoughtlessly of truths which we need, that there may not come such demoralization of opinion and practice as to put back in our time the cause for which all times and all providences have contributed, it may be well to consider some of the plain Conditions of Belief.

1. Doctrines that plainly honor God are commended to our faith. Many religions degrade the divine Being. All forms of paganism make the god only equal to the best, or perhaps less than the worst, of men. "The worshiper, carried through the long avenues of columns and statues and the splendid halls of the ancient temple of the Egyptian Thebes, was conducted at last to a miserable termination, when in the inner shrine he found one of the lower animals." A worship that finds its finality in a brute can hardly excite our contempt, so much does it deserve our pity. The old mythologies placed in the seats of the gods personages who were stained with the vices and crimes of those who inaugurated them. Those who accepted their teachings worshiped men only who were more degraded than themselves.

Much of the assumed science of our day would utterly dethrone God. It imputes the order of nature to impersonal force. The changes that have been wrought through the ages it would account for by a dominant and universal principle

of evolution.   It finds life in the material atoms.
The wide and splendid and manifold phenomena
lead back only to law.   It sees no need and recog-
nizes no evidence of God.   So we are thrown
back upon blank atheism.   This is nothing new.
One by one, as the natural sciences have emerged
into the realm of thought, they have at first been
considered as hostile to Biblical doctrine, but as
broader reaches of the facts have been gained, the
hostility has disappeared.

All science needs to be builded on the broadest
possible basis.   He who runs into conclusions, as
against a personal Creator or the Bible, before he
is thoroughly satisfied with his own science, ac-
knowledges his own unwisdom.   Over and over
again has the apothegm of Lord Bacon been verified: "A little philosophy makes a man an atheist.
A deeper study of it brings him back to God."
The mind is the chief factor in interpretation,
whether of Scripture or of nature.   The influences
which work upon it for evil or for good are often
invisible and undetected, and only the result will
show whether it was open or closed to all the
voices of God, and to all the methods by which
he works for the union of the soul to himself.

Professedly Christian instructors, too, have fostered meager conceptions of God by what they
have propounded concerning him.   A God who
does not look with aversion upon sin, while he

may pity and seek to save those who commit it, is not a God fit for us. Teachings which represent him as sanctioning practices which are abhorrent to a rightly educated conscience can be safely rejected. The authority of a creed which sets forth God's approval of what good men would consider crimes, or what wise men would consider follies, may well be denied. Our faith is challenged, first of all, by that which honors God. He must be enthroned above human imperfections, with a character whose alpha and omega is holiness. A God countenancing sin, in league with whatever spoils human happiness on the one hand, or diminishes his own purity on the other hand, is not the being for us to worship. Here it is that the God of the Bible outranks the imaginary divinities. Philosophy stands abashed before revelation. Here One is made known to us worthy of our regard, our reverence, our love. The Bible honors God: it exalts him to a throne, brilliant, glorious. It never lowers the divinity to us, but draws us up to adore him whose character and whose works are altogether such as to inspire right sentiments in us.

2. Truth, to demand our faith, must be announced through credible and reputable mediums. It would not be consistent with the acknowledged character of God for him to employ wicked or contemptible agents to make known to men the

great facts which are vital to their happiness and
holiness.   Any doctrine therefore which comes to
us through such channels may well be set aside
as lacking an essential element in the conditions
of belief.

We may properly demand of him who claims
to have a new revelation a palpable, public miracle as assurance that he is sent from God.   And
the miracle must be wrought not in the presence
of interested disciples and in the dark, but openly
before the multitude.   It must be, not a pretended
sign, devised for effect on the uninitiated, but a
real, benevolent work, witnessed by those who are
capable of judging of its genuineness and intent.
He who works it must be a good man, with an
established character for honesty and uprightness.
It is supposable that a man might be in league
with the devil and that communications might be
received from him which would be strange to those
of us who are ignorant of his devices.

We must, therefore, demand that revelators shall
be worthy of such an office, men whom God
would be likely to commission for such an important duty.   They need not be rich men, nor those
high in place and power, but they must be good
men, whose character is above suspicion.   The
prophets and apostles, who were inspired by the
Holy Spirit, were humble men for the most part,
whose personal influence did not spring from their

external position, but whose personal character challenged respect and whose words were therefore with power. But this principle effectually silences our modern revelators, the pretended promulgators of new faiths. In many cases they have not the personal qualities which command even the respect of men, and they are far from being such persons as we should naturally infer the divine Being would select to inform men of truth essential to their salvation. We object to the mediums; we say that many of them are more likely to be the agents of the devil than of the Deity. Though there may be among them good men, with souls that are easily moved to accept of any new or wonderful thing, yet the foremost of them, in any fair judgment, are not men of God. We therefore scout their assumptions. If we ask for miracles, they are powerless to invoke the interposition of higher laws. Signs fail. The imposture is palpable. Better mediums must be procured before intelligence will recognize the authority of the modern setters forth of new doctrine. On this ground the religion of the Bible stands preeminent. They were holy men who were moved by the Holy Spirit.

3. Doctrines in which all the Scriptures harmonize are worthy of our assent. Anything can be made out of detached portions of the Bible. Any monstrous dogma or heresy can be fortified within isolated paragraphs or texts of Scripture.

There is a sentence which declares, " There is no
God." But it is essentially modified by what pre-
cedes it. " The *fool* hath said in his heart, There
is no God." The inability of the sinner to obey
the commands of God can be gathered from texts
like this: " The mind of the flesh . . . is not subject to the law of God, neither indeed can it be."
But we learn what kind of an inability it is when
we read these words of Christ, " Ye will not come
to me, that ye may have life." The fact that
Christ died for the elect is plainly taught by some
passages, but the doctrine of a limited atonement
is utterly overthrown when we bring to bear upon
it such passages as these:—" He is the propitiation
for our sins; and not for ours only, but also for
the whole world;" " That by the grace of God
he should taste death for every man." There is a
large class of texts which speak of the future destruction of the wicked, which teach that they shall
utterly perish. Some have inferred from this
strong language that the finally impenitent are to
be annihilated. But another class of texts, which
speak of the endless existence of the wicked in a
state of consciousness, obliges us to give such meaning to the former texts that both shall harmonize.
Such a meaning is obvious. As the life of the
righteous is eternal well-being, so the destruction
or death of the wicked is eternal ill-being. In that
meaning all the Scripture harmonizes, and in no

other. Awful as the truth is, hard as it may be to believe it, we must accept it or reject the Bible. If the Scriptures are authoritative with us, that meaning, in which their combined texts on any subject harmonize, must be received as the truth of God, or else we are afloat on a boundless sea of conjecture and doubt.

4. Truth that bears against ourselves, as accountable beings, is probably commended to our belief. Such truth is unpalatable to the unrenewed or the partially sanctified nature. Men like to think well of themselves, and to have others think well of them. They do not like hard doctrines which humble their pride and refute their self-righteousness. They put their morality high, a great deal higher than God does. They enumerate their good deeds with Pharisaic content. They look down on sinners beneath themselves. Certain texts they would read out of the Bible. They cannot think it will go as hard with them as such passages would indicate. Hence come forms of religionism designed to make it easy for men to go through the world and to meet the issues of probation, to give substitutes for Biblical orthodoxy and godly repentance and humble faith in Christ and a holy, self-denying, cross-bearing life. God's terms are set aside. This may be according to the pleading of human nature, but it is not according to the gospel of

Christ. The better way is to take the worst possible view of ourselves, or rather, to look at ourselves just as we are, which is very much the same thing, and then seek deliverance. If we are sinners, we do not change that fact by calling ourselves saints nor by requiring others to call us so. If the wrath of God abides on us, we shall not shake it off by thanking him that we are not as other men are. If there are truths that bear hard upon us, that show us to ourselves in a bad light, we shall probably not go far amiss if we insert these truths in our creeds. The presumption is that the statements do not come up to the reality. The sinner, moved by the Holy Spirit to look at himself as he is, feels that the half has not been told; his pungent convictions sometimes beget despair. If he gains relief, it is not by thinking any better of himself, but by learning to trust in Christ as a Saviour for the lost. A stupid self-conceit is not an honest judgment of one's self. The Biblical doctrines that humble us, that spoil the self-glory of our hearts, that direct us as lost sinners to the only way of escape, the blood of an atoning Saviour, are those which are most worthy of our acceptance, though their very truthfulness may repel us from them.

5. Those truths should be embraced in our belief which are safe in any event. The possibilities should be considered in important de-

cisions. The statesman in peace will prepare for war. The mariner is best off who has provided for storm. The business man is strong who can bear up under the possible failure of his securities. In the great matters of the soul and eternity, when opposing doctrines are presented for credence, it is well to accept those which, if there is room for question, in any event are safe. Take, for illustration, the two leading doctrines of the future state of those who go out of this world in unbelief, —first, that the finally impenitent are to be consigned to misery without end; secondly, that all men, whatever their character or conduct, are to be at last universally saved. He who accepts the former of these doctrines and acts in the light of it, by flying to Christ as a Saviour from coming wrath, is safe in either event. If all are saved, he is saved; if some are lost, he is not among them. How is it with him who holds the latter and who has no Saviour? What if he has embraced the wrong doctrine? What if the future should be quite otherwise? What if the Bible statement of "torment forever and ever" should prove to be true? He has committed a fatal mistake. He has done himself infinite harm. He has before him a fearful harvest. This should be a primal condition of belief, that those doctrines should be embraced which are safe in any event.

It is not a small thing what we believe. God

will hold us accountable for our beliefs and for the
actions which flow from them.   Nor is the right
faith a difficult matter to gain, if we approach the
evidences with the teachable disposition.

Great, solemn truths are revealed to us.   We
are in charge of eternal verities.   The science of
God and of man, of sin which is lithographed on
the globe, and of salvation which is written in the
blood of Calvary, of probation and of the enduring destinies, is all brought within our cognizance.
We have the knowledge of Christ and of his gospel, of the blessed fact which steadies the rolling
world on its uneasy orbit, that there is salvation
for the lost.   Life and immortality are brought to
light.   We know that heaven or hell is before us.
Facts large enough and important enough to make
our life serious, and our work here momentous,
are in our possession.   As far as we can judge,
they are *verified* facts.   They have entered into
the life and history of ages.   They belong to man,
as responsible and immortal.   They are taught by
the inspired Word.   They are confirmed by human
experience.   They have been voiced in song and
prayer, which have alternately expressed the hope
and fear, the penitence and aspiration, of souls.
They have not been abandoned in death.

And what would the world be without them,
and what would man be if he lost faith in them?
The babblings that are profane and vain, the oppo-

sition of science falsely so called, must not rob us
of immortal birthrights. We cannot give up these
eternal certainties for the guesses of whatever dis-
coverer. We cannot let go of a divine hand to
grasp we know not what. We cannot degrade
ourselves to brutish origin or kindredship, when
our aspirations are beyond the skies and to the
seats of angels.

If the universe had a Creator, and if he
impressed his laws upon it and is the governor of
that which he wisely made, he challenges our undoubted allegiance. If in this world of sin, sin so
palpable that it stares in our faces everywhere,
there is a divine redemption so that every lost man
may be saved, it were only folly and presumption
either to ignore or reject it. We cannot accept
charlatanry for Christianity. Not yet can we
throw overboard chart and compass and reckon-
ings and commit ourselves to the turbulence of a
sea swept by hurricanes and thundering on a coast
white with the foam of breakers. We must have
something to go by; something that will hold.
What is it? Speculation? Uncertain science?

Undoubtedly an age of skepticism and materialism degrades the conditions of belief. Sacredness
is at a discount. All things are common and
cheap. When the soul is resolved into a breath,
and God into a myth, there is no room for consecration and no object in effort. The blow that

dethrones God dethrones man.   All great things
go down together.   Life runs to commonplace.
A new fascination comes to worldly business, and
young and ambitious men feel it.   To gain the
world, to hold its wealth and the power which
wealth gives, to feel that the vast systems of
commerce and trade which vex the seas and jar
the land are tributary to their plans, and that they
are the moneyed kings on whose confidence
thrones stand, on whose vote republics succeed in
the throes of revolutionary struggle, whose power
is greater than that of armies and navies, in whose
counting-rooms destiny is dictated, is something
wonderfully alluring.

The same conditions give an equal, though different fascination to the studies of nature.   To
unlock the palaces that have been closed and
guarded for countless ages, to let light in upon
their splendors and to stand first of all, first of a
line of mind-kings, amidst their regal glories, to
hear the majestic minstrelsies, the old choruses,
that have reverberated there with no ear to listen ;
to discover the laws, ancient as the globe, written
by the divine finger on tables of stone laid up
there as in arks of testimony ; to detect the fine
arts of nature, its pictures and sculptures and
traceries and tapestries and the consummate grace
and glory of its architecture ; to lead the way of
exploration through rooms and galleries where no

human foot has trodden before, possesses a charm which carries brave students through endeavor and sacrifice. We admire and approbate the steady devotion, the unyielding faith and constancy, of those leaders of thought. The scientific ranks are crowded with noble minds which in every step of their progress win our love.

But the questions of responsibility and of destiny are profounder than those of business and of science. We demand the higher estimate for that which affects the soul and reaches through the eternities. We enter a protest against the materialistic tendency •and against the scientific unbelief and against the vice of worldliness. We maintain the enthronement of God and the authority of Holy Scripture, and the central place in the world of the cross of Christ. We ask that the tremendous issues of the future shall not be slighted nor travestied nor handed over to blind and unsatisfactory ignorance. We want those verities which have wrought on human character for the sturdiness and uprightness of our fathers still to be among the active forces of philosophy and society.

On the high tablelands of the Andes, among the mountains that tower above Quito, where the old Indian race, driven back from the sea, driven out and back from their ancient seats and capitals, still holds its own in the free air and under the free skies, and within the impregnable fastnesses of the eternal hills, as it is said, lies a gorgeous city which they have builded and maintained, while below and around them the overwhelming tide of conquest has passed. There they have kept their greatest ancestral inheritance. Father to son has transmitted the secret of the rich mines and no one has ever betrayed them. There the old architecture rises in its strange glory, and roofs and battlements glitter with gold and flashing gems.

To us has come down a grander inheritance. Shall we as faithfully transmit and guard it, and shall our treasures of thought and love be builded into that city which is lightened by the glory of God?

V

PARTICULARITY OF CHRIST'S MESSAGE

"And Peter,"—*Mark* 16 : 7.

———

At Bethlehem, N. H.

Christ has a particular message for each soul. It is as though he called each one by name and laid on him, personally, the burden of duty.

He has a message for all the world: great mankind-calls; comprehensive world-truths; proclamations to all the nations, and for all the ages. He draws the world unto himself. He was the true Light, which lighteth every man coming into the world; and his invitations and his commands are for all souls.

But beside them, he has a word, a special utterance, a significant invitation, to each person, adapted to that person more than to any other, holding a meaning for him which it would not exactly hold for any other. "Go, tell his disciples *and Peter.*"

Peter was one of Christ's earliest and most trusted and intimate disciples. He had been with the Master throughout all his public life. He was one of the three who had been admitted to the greatest intimacy and privacy with our Lord; before whom Jesus had been transfigured, when his face did shine as the sun, and his garments became white as the light; with whom he had gone into the gloom and terror of Gethsemane when his soul was exceeding sorrowful, even unto death; who had been suffered to accompany him when he raised from the dead the daughter of the ruler of the synagogue. He had been under the private instruction of the great Teacher, and knew his character and his purposes. His house, on the shore of the lake at Capernaum, had been the rendezvous of the disciples, in which the miraculous power of the Healer had been wonderfully shown.

He was a typical Galilæan; with worldly ambitions, fond of change, ready to embark in new enterprises, susceptible to new impressions, quick to draw the sword on occasion, forward to speak and to follow his words with corresponding actions. It was Peter who asked, with proud aspiration, "What then shall we have? *We*, who have left all and followed thee?" He kept his eye on the main chance, and wanted no low place in the coming kingdom. He had the worldly idea of the Messiahship. It was Peter who, as the night of agony in Gethsemane approached, courageously said, "Even if I must die with thee, yet will I not deny thee." It was Peter who, as the traitors closed around his Lord, quickly drew his sword and smote the servant of the high priest and struck off his ear. It was Peter who followed the captors

even into the court of the high priest's palace, to
see the end.

And it was Peter, too, who denied his Lord,
denied him once, and again, and the third time;
and swore to the falsehood.   So inconsistent, con-
tradictory, unreliable, was this strong, weak man;
afraid of no soldier, cringing before a maid.   Yet
he was Peter, the Rock; so that his personal faithfulness of confession became the rock on which
the eternal Church should be builded, and against
which the forces of hell should not prevail.   It was
Peter who confessed, "Thou art the Christ, the Son
of the living God."   It was Peter who worshiped
him, saying, "Of a truth thou art the Son of God."
It was Peter who answered him, "To whom shall we
go? thou hast the words of eternal life."   This man
had the courage of his convictions.   He had the
capabilities of a grand manhood.   He was fitted
for devoted attachment.   He would identify himself with his Master.   He would make the cause
which he had espoused the passion of his life.   He
would consecrate himself and all that he had to
the propagation of the kingdom, to the conquering
sweep of the gospel and its proclamation to Gentiles
as well as to Jews.

Christ measured the man.   He knew all men,
and he needed not that anyone should bear witness concerning man; for he himself knew what
was in man.   He knew this man.   He knew what

was in him, what splendid possibilities were as yet
undeveloped in him, what a rock he would be for
the infant Church, with what a fearless eloquence
he would proclaim the gospel, with what undaunted
boldness he would face the enemies of his Lord.

Christ might have rejected him.   He had denied
Christ.   He deserved to be rejected, as many of us
do.   We have not always been true to our Master.
But the Master loved the disciple; he could for-
give and forget the sin of the penitent disciple who
wept bitterly over his folly and sin.   He knew
that in spite of this shameful denial there was stuff
in him for a great apostle and for a fearless martyr.

And so, after he had risen from the dead, when
he was turning to his true friends that he might lay
on them the burdens and responsibilities and vast
interests of his kingdom, he instructed his mes-
senger to say, " Go tell his disciples and Peter,"
and especially Peter.

The after life of this great apostle proved that
the Lord was not mistaken in him.   Almost at the
very time when these words were spoken, he was
on his way to the vacant sepulcher, which he was
the first to enter.   He was the first of the apostles
to whom the risen Christ appeared.   With deepest
humility and affection he three times replied to the
three times repeated question, " Lovest thou me? "

Before the haughty Jews, in the face of their
pitiless tribunals, he proclaimed Christ as the

Messiah of their nation and of the world.   He
stood at the head of the apostles, and was their
leader in the great work which was upon their
hands.   It was Peter, on the day of Pentecost,
when Jerusalem was full of men from every nation
under heaven, whose voice was lifted up to declare
to the assembled people the resurrection of Jesus
Christ from the dead and that he was both Lord
and Christ.   It was Peter who, when the multitude
were convicted, preached the new doctrine of
repentance and acceptance in the name of Jesus
Christ; and on that day three thousand of his
hearers received the word and were added to the
disciples.

It was Peter who wrought the first apostolic miracle: when a lame man at the door of the temple
which is called Beautiful asked alms of the apostles
and Peter, with undoubting confidence in the power
of the Master, said to him: "Look on us. . . . In
the name of Jesus Christ of Nazareth, walk."   It was
Peter who improved the occasion of that miracle on
that day, and on the next day, boldly to preach
the doctrine of the crucified Christ as the only one
through whom salvation can be gained.   For, he
said, " Neither is there any other name under heaven,
that is given among men, wherein we must be
saved."

So all along in the history you will see that it
was Peter who stood in the forefront of the gospel

preachers, challenging the enemies of Christ to their duty and claiming that he must speak the things that he had seen and heard. The sick caught the magic of his name and lay along the streets on beds and couches, that as Peter came by, at the least his shadow might overshadow some one of them.

It was Peter who was brought forth by night out of the prison, where the priests had caused him to be confined and was reported to them in the morning as standing in the temple and teaching the people ; and who, when he was brought before the council, said to them : "We must obey God rather than men." It was Peter who early entered upon evangelical tours, carrying forth the gospel into Samaria, to Syrophœnicia, to Lydda, Joppa, and Cæsarea. He was the first to receive the heathen into the Christian Church, and by his wide missionary journeys first gave the missionary character to the world-embracing and world-conquering faith.

Christ made no mistake in respect to this man. He knew that his great work needed just the qualities that Peter had. And he made use of them for the honor of the disciple and the glory of the Master. The world owes much to this apostle. He gave character to the rising and growing Church. He has been an example for these centuries suited to all ministers and missionaries, to all

followers of Christ. There was vast meaning in
the message: "Go tell the disciples and Peter."

So we come back to the truth with which we
started of the particularity of Christ's message to
each individual.

We may notice, in the first place, that every
man has his particular qualities, aptitudes, characteristics. No two men are exactly alike. No two
leaves, blades of grass, flowers; no two gems,
rubies, diamonds; no two animals; no two faces,
features, are precisely similar. Peter was not at all
like John; he could not be mistaken for James.
You never think of him as being any one but
Peter. The artists, in aiming to reproduce on
canvas the apostles of Christ, give Peter an expression, a personality, quite unlike any one of the
others. With a massive head, a beetling brow,
eyes in which lightning flashes, he has also a frame
of strength, and looks like a man fitted to be the
leader of armies. Among the strong men of the
apostleship, he has a unique personality.

So every man, when he is known, when his
qualities and characteristics are subjected to anal-
ysis, is only himself and not any one else. In a
deep, true sense, he stands alone.

He was made to be himself. If he goes about
to make himself some one else, to be like some
other man, to try to wear clothes that were made
for a very different person, to fit himself into a

place that was designed for some one a great deal
smaller or a great deal larger than he is, he makes
a great blunder, to speak mildly of it, and we
might almost call it a crime. For is it not, in effect, charging God with a mistake? Is it not, in
effect, claiming that he ought to be, ought to have
been made to be, another person than he is?
Now God makes no mistakes. His molds are divine.

Such as he made you, with the endowments
that you have, with the qualities of mind and body
that you possess, he has a personal message for
you. For he knows you thoroughly. Men may
not know you so. They may have an idea that
they understand your make-up. But how often
are they deceived! The man who knows how to
speak the right word to another, the word that fits
his case, is the man who has power over the other.
A man of keen mind was examining the work of
a schoolboy. The boy was discouraged, almost
despairing. The man noticed one thing which the
timid boy half hid. It was his drawing. He saw
in that the elements of mastery; the signs of
genius. He frankly told the boy of his power and
stimulated his aspiration. The student came to
him afterward privately and asked him if he meant
it. He replied that he certainly did. He spoke
to the boy's true self. Other men, teachers, had
mistaken him, had not understood what was in him.

But here was a voice of sympathy and understanding that roused the slumbering soul, that thrilled on the sensibilities of a talented mind, as the hand of a master will draw sweetest music from a well-made harp. That boy became a renowned artist. God knows who you are, and he speaks to you such as you are. He knows exactly your framework, for his forming hand fashioned it. He knows your mental qualities, for by his breath you became a living soul.

In the second place, these particular aptitudes and characteristics are to be taken account of in the discipline of life. Education is *leading out* that which is in one. True education includes finding out what is in one and then making the most of it. The higher education runs much to *electives*. The student, by the aid of his instructors, is assumed to find out what he is fitted for; then he applies himself to those studies which develop what is in him. If he is possessed of a talent for language, he strives for success along that line and becomes learned in the tongues of the world. If he has a natural gift for philosophy, he does not lose the advantage of it by working poorly at physics. A good farmer should not be spoiled for the sake of making a poor lawyer. It indicates civic degradation when the judicial bench is occupied by a saloon-keeper. Statesmen are not raised from down-grade politicians.

All men are not made for the same end.   Some
are designed for one station, others for a different
station.   One star is made for a sun ; another for
a planet;   another for the satellite of a planet.
Nor are men to be wrought on by the same
methods for the places for which they are
designed.   They are to be developed according to
their material.   Marble is to be wrought into a
statue by the chisel.   Iron is to be wrought into a
statue by melting and molding ; wood, by the
knife and plane.

God would have his creations become wise,
holy, efficient.   He would have them eminent in
his service according to their several ability.   He
does not expect Peter to be Paul.   It is rarely
that one could be a Luther.   Edwards had the
material which few men possess.   Through influence of one kind Calvin became what he was.
Through conditions peculiar to him Wesley was
fitted for his missions.   History traces it to inci-
dental circumstances that the founder of Metho-
dism and the hero of Waterloo pursued such different courses.   But divine Providence was in it.
The hand of the Almighty wrought on them.

The particular qualities and aptitudes of men
are taken account of in the discipline by which
they are trained and qualified for their work ; by
which they are led to be such as they become.

God is a master builder.   He knows what the

material is upon which he works. He knows into
what it may be fashioned by the agencies which
he uses for the building of immortal souls. He
misunderstands no man. He makes no mistake
as to inherent characteristics or as to possible
results. So he has a particular message for
each one. He calls every man to his place.
He points out the path for every foot. He directs
the personal exertion which each one needs to
make.

It is for every man to heed God—to put himself into personal accord with his guide and
Saviour.

In the third place, men need particular appeal,
personal influence, special encouragement. Peter
was in that condition that he needed something
special, specific, said to him and done for him.
And the Master knew this when he said, "Tell
the disciples *and Peter.*" He knew, indeed, the
want of that apostle better than the apostle himself knew it. How thoroughly, how tenderly, he
met it! And how successfully! And how per-
manent was the lesson! Peter became another
man; of the same qualities, indeed, but differently
directed and accomplishing different results. From
that time he led the conquests of the kingdom.

Every man has an approachable side. There is
a joint in every man's harness through which an
arrow can be shot. Men have their weak points

and their strong points.   A strong man once
made a study of a friend for months that he might
learn how to gain him, and learning that, he
brought his friend to Christ.

On what line shall the appeal be 'made?   Christ
had one word for Nathanael, and a different one
for Nicodemus; one word for the woman of
Samaria, and a different one for Mary Magdalene.
Study the quality and the characteristics of one
whom you would lead to the Master; of one
whom you would win from sin, from indulged
habits of impenitence, and bring over to godliness
and Christian service.

Find out, if you can, by what influence you can
convert a neighbor and save a soul from death.
That which would take hold of one man would
repulse another man.   One motive is commanding, another motive is futile, with a certain class of
minds.   One soul needs encouragement; another
needs warning.   One man is influenced by that
which appeals to his personal interests; another
by that which reaches to his family and his
friends.

God's word addresses every man.   Apply that
word with its particular appeal, persuasion, warning, encouragement, hope, to him whom you
would see in the kingdom.

Remember that there is a power back of yours;
that there is an incomprehensible influence exerted

on all minds to gain them if possible; and seek to
act in harmony with God.   God acts with immeasurable wisdom, as one who is acquainted with the
subject; and we are wise if we act with God.   Get
acquainted with the person, and so know what his
need is, what his weak point is, what his strong
point is, and bring your influence into coincidence
with the divine influence.   Always feel that God
is foremost; that where he leads you can safely
follow.   His awakening spirit must be first; your
corresponding effort must be harmonious with
him.   Make account of the difference in minds.

Tennyson, walking with some friends, tarried
behind to look into a brook.   When he overtook
them, he said, "What a wonderful imagination
God has!"   They passed the brook, seeing only
its rippling surface; he looked into its shallows
and saw there the work and the wonders of
Almightiness.

"And Peter."   You are Peter!   Christ has a
particular message for you.   Just where you are,
just what you are, he speaks to you.   It may be
a voice of tender warning that you may hear if
you will only listen.   You have gone far enough
on the path that you have chosen to walk in;
every step hereafter is full of peril.   If you would
escape the risk, would flee from danger, you will
heed his word to you.

It may be a voice of comfort.   You have suffered; you have borne heavy burdens; you have met great losses. He would console you, and by his hand of strength he would relieve you and make your evening of woe to be followed by a morning of joy, as the gloomiest night is often succeeded by the brightest dawn.

It may be a voice of instruction. You do not know what to do, which way to turn, how to escape the consequences of sin. He will give you specific direction, so plain that "the way-faring men, yea fools, shall not err therein."

You need not be lost. You may be saved. Warning, instruction, comfort, are freely spoken for you, to meet your special case. Christ, indeed, has a message for you as direct and specific as though you were the only man. He speaks, as I said, to all men; he gives a mankind-call. But he singles you out, as though he spoke your name, as though his message were for you alone.

Peter listened and obeyed. He consecrated his life, himself, to Christ, and he left the impress of his devotion and sacrifice on other lives, on the widening history of the Church, on the victorious kingdom of God. Peter followed Christ, and so he became the leader of many souls into the gates of light. The Galilæan fisherman became a "Fisher of Men."

Listen, my friends, as Peter listened, to the voice of the dear Christ. You may not hear him in the earthquake of popular financial trouble, nor in the whirlwind of political agitation, but he will speak by a still, small voice to your very soul. It may be as you in solitude read his Holy Word; it may be as you feel the anguish and loneliness of an inconsolable sorrow; it may be as the Holy Spirit himself convinces you of your inexpressible need; it may be in the solemn providences that darken your pathway. But in whatever way he speaks, it is as a loving Friend, as a divine Redeemer.

7

VI

VICARIOUS SUFFERING

".. Even as the Son of man came not to be ministered unto, but to minister, and to give his life a ransom for many."

Matthew 20 : 28.

On the Dedication of the Chapel of the Christian Commission, at Point of Rocks, Virginia.

VICARIOUS SUFFERING

The experiences of these eventful times are giving new meaning and fresh force to old and familiar truths.

Voices, tenderer and more strong than any whose tones break out from all the past, solemnly urge them upon our attention, and events of tragic and transcendent import are interpreting them to our hearts as they have heretofore been interpreted to the cold and unresponsive reason. *Rebellion* was always a black word in the language, and it meant more or less to those who carelessly pronounced it. But spoken in the lurid light of the flames that it has kindled over one half of our beloved land, amidst the agonies of a people struggling for their very life, with the awful memories of its accursed work on battle-fields piled with the dead, and in homes made desolate forever, and on hearts broken by its murderous blows it gleams with a fearful significance, and includes in its contents all that is worst in earth and in hell.

Loyalty always sounded with a sweet tone, whether it described an individual or a people;

but illuminated by the devotion of those heroes of our own, who during these last years have cheerfully offered their lives for their land, by the enlistment of our noble volunteers, who have sacrificed all dearest objects, chosen pursuits, study, home, parents, wife, children, for the defence of their country, it beams with a luster rivaled by no other word in all human speech, and suggests the lofty love of heaven! Sublime were those last words of a wounded general (Robert McCook) to a friend, "I am done with life; yes, this ends it all. You and I part now, but the loss of ten thousand lives such as yours and mine would be nothing if their sacrifice would but save such a government as ours."

The great central truth of Christianity, *the vicarious atonement of Christ*, the voluntary offering of the Son of God for the sins of the world, for the salvation of sinners, stands out in bolder relief on the background of events which are now transpiring, the offerings of precious lives, the sacrifices of loyal hearts, for the salvation of our beloved country.

We can appreciate now, as we never could before, the work of the Redeemer for us. Our hearts warm toward him with a truer love, our thanks ascend to him with a more intelligent earnestness, for his humiliation and his death in our behalf, when we see them enforced and made real by the tribulations through which we are passing. The deaths of those who have fallen on all our memorable battle-fields, the patient endurance of the sick and wounded in hospitals, the unwearied devotion of mothers and sisters, which survives all hardships and loneliness and affliction, the prolonged agonies of a whole people, among whom every circle has been invaded, and in all whose homes the voice of mourning has been heard, all draw us to Christ, suggest his greater endurances, and bow us in gratitude at his cross. " Even as the Son of man came not to be ministered unto, but to minister, and to give his life a ransom for many."

Perhaps I cannot choose a better theme for our thought to-day than this old doctrine of *vicarious suffering*, made a living truth by the stirring history of the present. By vicarious suffering, I mean that suffering which is endured for others. And such is a large proportion of all the woe of the world, not for the sufferer's sake, but in behalf of others. Our blessings are the result of others' burdens. Every pleasure has been purchased by another's pain. Throughout all history, in every age and every land, stands prominently forth this doctrine of substituted suffering. It flows in all the blood that has been shed; it flames in every martyr fire; it speaks in the dying testimony of confessors; it is eloquent in the speech of patriots

who have fallen; it is commemorated by historic
battle-fields; it follows the footsteps of exiles; it
is written on prison walls; it hallows the endurance of peoples struggling against iron tyrannies;
it makes the cross the world's most sacred emblem;
it consecrates Gethsemane and Calvary.

Let me bring to your notice the causes of this
strange and sublime phenomenon:

I. The interlinkings of the social state require it.
We stand not in the world apart, each man an
entire being by himself, independent and unaf-
fected by others' weal or woe. But we are all
linked together—one mighty, mysterious chain of
being, along which the electric current, communi-
cated at one point, flashes and thrills, until the
whole has felt the shock to which any part has
vibrated. The first blow fell, slight, awful, stun-
ning not those alone on whom it fell then, but all
who came after them as well, so robbing a race of
its glory, and laying it under the spell and curse
of sin.

Society is made up of parts, fitted to each other
as the blocks of a massive structure are fitted and
cemented together. Standing in order and strength
all is well, but let there be a displacement of a
single block, and there is a weakening and a crum-
bling and a falling of the whole in one melancholy
ruin.

Look first at the family, the earliest and the

best of the social relations. There substituted suffering has its appointed place. It comes in the
adjusting of human hearts that must beat together.
It comes in the strange mystery of birth, in all
the pain of the mother for her child. It comes in
weary watchings and anxieties, as the child passes
through successive periods of peril. It comes in
the sickness that startles with its awful shadow,
and its prophecy of heavier woe. It comes in the
changes which the years bring, of hope and despair,
of holiness and depravity, of sweet, maturing life, of
dark, miserable being. It comes in wrestlings and
cries of wounded hearts at the mercy-seat for way-
ward children of the covenant, in disappointments
worse than death, and in burdens heavier than those
of age. God hears no sadder voices than those
which go up from pious parents for apostate offspring; prayers, mingled with divine promises and
heavy human woes, bursting and gushing from
torn hearts. This is suffering of which those for
whom it is endured know little, often, alas! care
nothing.

Another endurance sometimes comes in the
family experience; that of the innocent child for
those who would, but cannot, relieve it. Like a
tender lamb, offered on the altar for the welfare of
all the family, the beautiful, winning child sickens,
suffers, dies. As the old Levitical code called for
the fairest of the flock, the choicest of the herd,

an offering without blemish and without spot, so
does God sometimes now call for the fairest of a
family, that by the sorrow and the suffering they
may be chastened for the life to come.   Well is it
when those who survive follow the Shepherd
up the heights to which he took their treasure.
There are flowers too sweet for our terrestrial gardens, and God transfers them to bloom under the
heavenly skies.   There are gems so pure that they
would dazzle our mortal sight, and God takes
them to shed their luster around his throne.   The
jewels that would be tarnished if left in our keeping are reserved in heaven for us, as crown jewels
are kept only for the coronation of kings.   Death,
as it thins the household, brings ever this experience of vicarious suffering.

Beyond the family, in the community and the
state, we find the same fact resulting from the
same causes.   There are those whose lot it is to
bear the burdens of the majority.   There are
those who stand forth preeminent among their fellow men as those who have suffered for all the
others.   Their names are luminous.   Their memory is sacred.   History embalms them in immortal urns.   Art, in its chiefest works, perpetuates
their features and their forms.   The world raises
them to enduring thrones.   The principles which
are the best, the blessings, social and political,
which are most prized, have not been a spontane-

ous growth, an easy harvest. They are the fruit of seed sown in tears, and enriched with the choicest blood and garnered by the agony of noble men.

Take the single, simple principle of the right of private judgment. For that what endurance has there been, what toil, what pain of body and of mind! What enjoyment has been renounced, what sacrifices have been made, what persecutions have been voluntarily endured! Reformers have stood up for it against authority and frowns and anathemas. Strong men have unsheathed the sword in its defence, and blood has flowed in torrents for its maintenance—a gory baptism of a sacred truth! Martyrs have offered up life for it; pilgrims have forsaken home and native land and sought new homes in strange climes for the sake of it. Europe rocked once in the strife for it. We hold it—a costly heritage—bequeathed through the *suffering* of noble forefathers.

Take the great cause of human freedom. We enjoy it. Our noble Northern land blooms in the light of it. Its opulent cities, its magnificent improvements, its schools and churches, its manufactures and its commerce, its science and art, its beautiful homes, its intelligent laws, and its cultured people, are its grandest memorials. But it cost something to secure it. In other lands, in ages long gone, the conflict and the suffering went on. Patriots sprang to its defence. Tell and

Wallace and Cromwell and Hampden and other goodly men led the hosts who battled for it. The closet, the prison, the battle-field, testified for it. On our shores our fathers spared not themselves, but, by marvelous endurance, prolonged and against multiplied hostilities, they secured it for us. Not for himself did Washington enter upon the struggle for our independence. He might have been a British noble, but he spurned the bribe which was offered to him, choosing rather to suffer for his people than to enjoy personal emoluments.

> " When Freedom, on her natal day,
> Within her war-rocked cradle lay,
> An iron race around her stood,
> Baptized her infant brow in blood,
> And, through the storm which round her swept,
> Their constant ward and watching kept.
>
> Our fathers to their graves have gone,
> Their strife is past—their triumph won ;
> But sterner trials wait the race
> Which rises in their honored place—
> A moral warfare, with the crime
> And folly of an evil time."

This greater revolution, in the throes of which we are travailing, and whose annals will dim our natal struggle, as they will all other heroic struggles of great peoples for their life, both by the

magnitude of the physical forces engaged and by
the sublimity of the moral end to be attained, is
calling for an amount of vicarious suffering which
will make our land the altar of the world.   These
mighty armies of our noblest brothers, moving
into the perils of protracted war, from which so
many will be offered ; these steady, trustful hearts
back of them, in all the homes that are lonely
because they are away, which daily, hourly, bear
up our sacrificing soldiery in prayer to God, and
which are almost broken by the tidings which
crash in upon them, these all are enduring for the
welfare of others.   For their children, for their
native and adopted land, for the populations that
are, in all the future, to enjoy what they have so
dearly purchased, all these freely suffer.   And
more will do it.   Other hearts will bring their
chiefest treasures, other lives will present their
costly devotion, so that this government shall
stand.   Such a sacrifice shall be made, so illustrious and so precious that the memory of it shall
be topmost in the history of mortal endurance,
shall stand forever next to the divine sacrifice of
the son of God for the redemption of the world.
Never will we let die, never will liberty-loving
men, in all nations, let die the memory of those
who give themselves as a ransom for this land.
Heroic literature, embalming their deeds in books,
shall be read by our children.   Art shall preserve

their record on canvas and in marble. A nation shall hold their names as its choicest treasures.

On a gravestone in Pennsylvania a mother has placed this inscription for her only son, who has fallen in this war: "A willing sacrifice to the great principle of liberty." On the southern coast a boat-load of loyal soldiers became exposed to the deadly fire of the enemy, the boat having run aground. It was necessary that some one should offer himself to save them. A colored man stepped forward, saying, "Somebody's got to die to get us out of this and it may as well be me." He then deliberately got out and pushed the boat into the stream, and fell into it pierced with five bullets. One of our noblest generals, General James C. Rice, in his last letter to his mother before the fearful battle of the Wilderness, in which he fell, wrote: "My Dear Mother: Good-by. We are going again to do our duty, to bravely offer up our life for that of the country, and through God we shall do valiantly."

With kindred devotion thousands on thousands have given themselves for the land they love. For us, for all who survive them, for all who shall come after them, in the golden ages that are to come as the fruit of their endurance, did they offer themselves as vicarious sufferers.

II. The demands of benevolence call for suffering in behalf of others. The wants and the woes of a burdened race make their touching appeal to those who can be moved by them, and who can do something to alleviate them.

The records of philanthropy catalogue a succession of names of honor of those who have not spared themselves that they might relieve the misery of others. Every great principle, every sublime truth, has had its martyred adherents. Every benevolent enterprise has been advocated at the cost of suffering. To lift men, guilty it may be, but human, out of their dark dungeons, the thousands must go down into the diseases and death that haunt them. It has not been without hazard that old wrongs have been redressed, great crimes been dragged to the light, ignominious institutions been assailed and overthrown, virtue and good ways been established and defended. Some must count not their lives dear to themselves, must give up the dearest privileges, must throw themselves into the perilous contest with their treasure and their blood, if others are to enjoy the blessing. Christ's cause in the world is a history of cheerful renunciation of all dearest things, of heroic self-denial and devotion and of personal suffering for others' welfare. His followers have walked in the painful footsteps of their Master, rewarded, no doubt, but still enduring the cross. "Even as the Son of man came not to be ministered unto, but to minister, and to give his life a ransom for many."

III. The necessity of the atonement for sin has
led to vicarious suffering. Sublime beyond all
other instances is that of the Son of God suffering
and dying in the place of sinners. All other
instances should only suggest to us this most marvelous offering, should only draw us nearer to the
cross. And if we suffer, if we take upon ourselves
the duty that involves loss and peril and sacrifice,
if we move forth to death in behalf of others, let us
bear in mind the agonies of the Redeemer for us,
and never forget that he gave his life a ransom for
us. In his case there was a necessity for the suffering as there could be in no other case. For unless he had undertaken for us there could have been
no salvation. If we shrink from duty for our fellow
men others may take the glory and the reward.
One only could bear the sins of the world. Would
God give up his beloved and only Son? Would
the Son of God become the Son of man, go down
into our lowliness, take up our sufferings and our
sin, become himself a sacrifice for us? It was so.
God gave his Son. Christ gave himself. He left
the throne for the humble manger. He left the
society of heaven for the society of sinners. He
left honor for shame, praise for cursing, glory for a
cross. We had sinned and so were lost. He
stood in our place before the law; he bare our sins
in his own body on the tree; he was wounded for
us; he died to save us. His chiefest title is

Saviour of sinners. He has done such a work for us that we can all be pardoned. He gave his life a ransom for man. His infinite life stands for all our forfeited finite lives. Now, if we will only believe, if we will only trust in him, if we will only consent that he shall be our Saviour, and love him and serve him, we may be saved. This is the gospel, the good news which we bring. We carry it to the camp and to the hospital; we whisper it to the dying warrior on the blackened ridges of battle and we announce it to the gathered soldiery in their peaceful assemblages. For this, that this gospel may be preached, we build and dedicate these tabernacles of worship amidst the camps of our noble armies. We love the brave men who stand as a wall of steel between our government and its enemies, and we would have them all love our Saviour.

As they peril their lives for their countrymen so Christ gave his life a ransom for them. To that Saviour so worthy of your affection, soldiers of the republic, we invite you now. We remind you anew of what he has done for you. We beseech you to give your manly strength, your worthy affection, to this divine Redeemer. As you have nobly heeded the call of the country, rallying under its flag, so enlist under the great Captain of our salvation, who can give you victory. As now, in our united prayer, we dedicate this chapel to his ser-

vice in worship, so in prayer dedicate yourselves
to him, and let this double offering be presented
to our Lord, the tabernacle and the worshipers in
it!

Many, my friends, are the instances during this
war, of the power and the value of religion in the
army and the navy. After the battle of Manassas
a colonel stood, like a brother, by a dying ser-
geant, and this was his testimony to his superior
officer: "Colonel, I am glad I am going to die;
I want to rest—the march has not been so long,
but I am weary—I am tired—I want to halt—I
want to be with Christ—I want to be with my
Saviour." To his sister and his aunt, who stood by
him he said: "Do not grieve: do not weep, for I
am going to Christ; I am going to rest in heaven."
"And, colonel," he said, with a brightening face,
"tell my comrades of the army, the brave Army
of the Potomac, that I died bravely, died for the
good old flag."

After the battle of Fort Donelson a dying officer
was asked what message he would send to his
friends, and his message was, "There is not a
cloud between me and Christ." After the same
battle a youthful soldier was seen sitting against
a tree while his life-blood gushed away and his
dying song was, "Nearer, my God, to thee."

A dear brother-in-law of mine, a captain in the
Fourteenth Connecticut, in this army, was mortally

wounded in one of the terrible battles of the Wilderness. He had carried his cheerful piety through marches and long compaigns and hard-fought battles, and into the prisons of Richmond; it remained with him in the sufferings of his last days, comforting the friends who gathered around him at Fredericksburg, and raying out upon brother officers and soldiers who loved him well and honored his consistent religious character. When he was asked by Bishop McIlvane if he regretted, lying there wounded and dying, that he had given himself to the cause of his country, he promptly replied: " No, bishop, if I had not been willing to give my life for my country I should never have entered the army." And when asked if he still trusted in Christ his answer was, " Living or dying my trust is in him alone." He spoke of heaven as a better country than this, and said, " Well, I shall be there and shall know all about it pretty soon." On the Sabbath morning of the day of his death he said, " To-day I shall get my marching orders; well, I am ready." In death victory was his, and he passed joyfully to that land of which he often spoke in fond anticipation, as alluring him by its grand realities.

The last words of Admiral Foote, of whom it was said during his Mississippi expedition, " He prays as though God did everything and fights as though man did everything," were, " I thank God

for all his goodness to me, for all his loving kindness to me; I thank him for his benefits." Renowned as was that brave naval officer, his greatest glory was his earnest Christian character.

One of our first astronomers, responding to the
call of his country when rebellion lifted itself
against the government, became a successful
leader of our armies. He had learned to look
beyond the stars, whose sublime pathways he had
traced, and devoutly to love Him who had made
them all, and when on our malarious Southern
coasts he was smitten with disease and saw that he
must die, General Mitchell said, "It is a blessed
thing to have a Christian's hope in a time like this!"
It detracts nothing from the heroic character of
that accomplished general who led the right wing
of the army in Sherman's triumphant march from
Atlanta to Savannah that he is known to be a
devoted Christian. Daily he gathers his military
family for worship. He bows in the meetings for
prayer, leading the devotions of the soldiers to Him
who alone giveth victory and peace. He kneels by
his dying soldiers and prays for them. It is told of
him that he entered the house where he learned a
soldier was dying, read to him from the words of
Christ, and prayed for him; then he bent down
and kissed him and said to him, "Captain G., we
shall meet in heaven!"

Such facts are the most precious in the records

of war. They gild its dark cloud with somewhat of the glory of heaven. I point you to these, a few out of many, to encourage you also to seek the faith which was such a strength and solace to them. Trust Him, O soldiers of the country, who, to you, living or dying, can give certain victory!

VII

FOR MEMORIAL DAY

"To grant unto us that we being delivered out of the hand of our enemies
"Should serve him without fear,
"In holiness and righteousness before him all our days."
—*S. Luke*, 1 : 74, 75.

MEMORIAL DISCOURSE IN GRAND AVENUE CHURCH, NEW HAVEN.

FOR MEMORIAL DAY

The highest patriotic spirit prizes political peace and prosperity as a means of enlarged spiritual growth and success. The result of victorious conflict in deliverance from the hand of our enemies should be the strengthening of holiness and righteousness among the favored people. War has its bitter experiences, but it has its useful lessons. Out of its carnage should come courage; out of its grime should come glory; through its travail and trial should be begotten noblest traits of character and heroic tests of conduct. The aspiration of the true patriot should be the inspiration of the true priest. Politics should be united to religion. The life of the nation should be made greater and grander by the death which has hallowed its history.

Once more we stand by the graves of the heroes. Once more, as we decorate the places where they sleep in silence, we hear the voices of their deeds and learn the lessons of their sacrificial lives. In the beautiful resurrection of nature their examples rise from out their graves, and we are charged to worthier ways of spending all our days.

It is not for the dead only that we observe the Memorial Anniversary. Nothing that we can do will affect them, for their work is nobly done and their record is forever closed. But in honoring their memory we can stimulate our fidelity; in recalling their service we can set ourselves anew to our responsible tasks.

Many years have passed since the tattered standards, borne back from successful battle, streamed along our streets, since the veterans, marching from bloody fields, passed in their last review before a grateful people. And those who are now coming into young manhood and womanhood can remember nothing of those great events which put a million of our noblest men into the field and furrowed our country with uncounted graves. It was one of the greatest wars of the world, if we estimate the principles that were involved in it and the land for whose future its battles were fought.

Our children should be reminded of the perils from which they have been delivered and of the debt they owe to the heroes who gave their precious lives to save the land and its liberties. But for the war they might have been with us still, contributing to the happiness of our homes and the welfare of our society. We can honor them by memorial services; we can honor them more by the service of worthy lives.

In the first place, in these memorial days, we may regard the war *as setting a true value to life*. War, in its very nature, necessitates the offering of many lives. War is contrived to kill as many as possible. That battle is considered as the most successful in which there has been the greatest number of the dead. War is costly in many ways, but it is most costly in lives.

Human life, therefore, is a principal element in all wars. What is life worth? What value can we fairly put upon it? Is life worth too much to be given up to armies and fightings, to the risks of camps and battle-fields?

Life is valuable for what it can worthily accomplish. Mere living has not any real worth. Mere living belongs to the brute creation, and in some sense to the vegetable production. But human life is the life of responsibility and influence. It is the life of being fashioned in the image of God and possessing immortality; of being endowed with reason, endowed with susceptibilities and with the power and freedom of choice; capable, therefore, of estimating values, of looking at motives, of feeling happiness and also remorse, and of determining personal character.

Each man of the two hundred thousand who fell in the defence of the Union—one hundred thousand on the field, one hundred thousand in hospitals or in wasting sicknesses at home—was

an accountable, influential, immortal soul. He
had but one earthly life to spend for some object.
That is all that any one of us has; one earthly
life, to be used in our way, according to our
choice, for such aim or object as we may select.
Those who went into the war for the Union with
intelligent appreciation of the act felt and knew
that they offered their lives for that cause. They
might go through safely. But they took the risk
of early and sudden death. They knew that in
the first great battle many would be stretched cold
and lifeless on the contested field. They knew
that they might be the first to fall; that the farewell which they had spoken to the dear ones at
home might be the last; and that they might look
no more on the faces of mothers and sisters and
fathers and brothers and wives and children.
They were willing to take the risk. Their country
called them. The land of their fathers, of their
birth, or their adoption—the land which held in it
many of the world's most precious hopes—was in
peril from treason and from armed enemies. They
sprang to its defence joyfully; students from their
books; men from all learned professions; merchants from their goods; artisans and farmers;
sacrificing all their plans, all their hopes, all their
old ambitions. Grand men stood in the ranks and
filled the camps.

I remember sleeping on the Potomac in a tent

that rang with college songs and college stories till midnight in the blaze of a fire of Virginia wood. I remember preaching in a chapel on the Appomattox that was filled with appreciative scholars and professional men. You could not live in the armies without knowing that you were in the midst of first-rate men. The lives of those who gave themselves to the defence of the country were among the most valuable we had to give. They knew the cost and they were willing to pay it. Wrote one of them from the field: " It is hard to be a private, hard to be an officer, hard to march, hard to fight, hard to be out on picket in the rain, hard to live on short rations and be exposed to all sorts of weather, hard to be wounded, hard to think of lying down in death without the gentle hand of love to smooth one's brow; but there is just one thing that makes all these things easy, and that is the spirit of Christian patriotism." That spirit lived in the armies. It sustained the soldiers through hardships and disappointments and defeats. It gave us victory and a country and our heroes.

The value of life is in its living. How are you living? How are you using the wonderful powers of your immortal soul? What is to be the record and the result? If you are living merely for yourself, for your present gratification, for the indulgence of low aims; if you are living in neglect of

duty and in denial of God, in carelessness for your
soul and your immortality, you put a low value on
life, on yourself.   Your life has value in so far as
you use it for great ends, for pure, true character,
for union with the living Christ, for the successful
entering on a blessed immortality.   As you stand
by the graves of the heroic dead, take a measure
of yourselves, gauge your lives, conclude that the
end will be what the immortality must be.

In the second place, we may regard the war *as
enthroning principle in affairs.*   There are many
downward tendencies in nations, as in individuals.
We need severe discipline to bring us back to the
true standard.   "Before I was afflicted I went
astray; but now I observe thy word," is the confession that follows the sorrows of many individuals.   It has its counterpart in national experience.
Perhaps there never was a time when our country
was in greater danger than during the years that
immediately preceded the war.   A sordid spirit
was abroad.   There was a truckling to expediency
on the part of public men.   Material prosperity
was the one desired end.   The national life was
honeycombed with greed and godlessness.   Our
foremost men bowed their necks to the yoke
of a domineering iniquity.   There was no great,
noble principle which pervaded the popular mind
and commanded loyalty.   Those who stood for
the right were stricken down, as Cæsar was

stricken down by Brutus. The floor of the senate
chamber was stained by the blood of its noblest
orator. The greatest statesman of our land was
ignobly held in moral shackles. The portents
were for evil. It seemed as though we were to
follow in the wake of accursed nations. Then the
war came. It came as the thunderbolt rives the
polluted air. It came as the hurricane sweeps
through malarious districts. It called the long
roll of all the people. It introduced a new motive.
It enthroned principle in affairs. It put right
uppermost. It gave new meaning to patriotism
and liberty. There was something worthy to be
fought for, even to die for. Men had lived for
selfishness and low-running ambitions. Now they
could die for sublime purposes. There was tonic
in the air. There was stimulus in speech. There
was new life for the nation.

It was a great thing that a people, not then a
century old in their organized independent national
being, should be arrested on the downward grade,
on which dead nations have slid to perdition, and
should be set with its face toward the sun in the
heavens! The war saved us. It gave us a new
atmosphere. It begot radical amendments in our
fundamental law. It revolutionized the constitution, and made of us a new people. I read one of
the latest utterances of one of our Connecticut sena-
tors, made during this current month in Congress:

"We say we were right. How are we ever going to decide? Some senator says, 'God only knows.' I bow reverently and admit it, but there are certain ways of arriving at that which must be accepted as right among men, and the last awful and great resort is the tribunal of war. We submitted to that, and we obtained that which we of the Union call right now; and so far as human laws and institutions and duties are concerned, we leave further judgment to the judgment day. So far as we, practically, are concerned, our side was and is right." This has the ring of the best days of old Connecticut. There is a Puritan throb and thrill in it. It is as though Sherman or Ellsworth spake.

Only last week I noticed the remark of a leading politician in respect to introducing a moral question into a political campaign, that the party could only be fully aroused to its duty when some great moral issue summoned it to the polls. And an influential political journal on the ground says in a late issue: "There is no public man in Kansas with either the courage or temerity to take the field as an avowed opponent of prohibition." The practical tests of our times are proving that there has been a new recognition of moral principle in the land ever since the war touched with its fingers of fire the conscience of the nation. We have a higher and purer public service. The interests of

morality are influential in legislation, and the
national conscience is sensitive.

In the third place, we may regard the war *as
accomplishing the purpose of Providence.* It is a
great thing to have God recognized. Nations
easily grow atheistic. Especially nations that are
successful come to confide in their power and
prosperity. Their material greatness looms before
their eyes, and shuts out all else. The roar of
their enginery drowns the thunder, and the march
of their progress distances Providence. They
need to be awakened. They need to be recalled
to first truths. When Abraham Lincoln issued
his Proclamation of Emancipation, he closed it
with the memorable words: "Upon this   .   .   .
I invoke the considerate judgment of mankind,
and the gracious favor of Almighty God." God
appeared then in our national life. There was
need of him. The human power was great and
terrible.

But there was need of a stronger arm. The
heavy battalions needed Omnipotence back of
them. From that time, when the nation wheeled
to the side of Providence, when the armies were
reinforced by the divine purposes, victories waited
on the Union flag. The work was immense. The
tides of war rolled with impetuous and awful fury
from the Mississippi to the Atlantic. Foote and
Farragut bombarded an open highway up and

9

down the Mississippi. Vicksburg fell before the
persistency of Grant. Thomas struck the vitals of
the Confederacy. Sherman swept a swath of desolation through the heart of the rebellious states.
The great armies of the Potomac and the James at
last reaped the fruits of their patient service, and
the history of the great rebellion was closed. The
prayers that had gone up from rice swamps and
cotton fields, borne on the plaintive and weird
cries and songs of slaves, had come to answering.
The faith of bold reformers, who had refused all
compromise with hideous oppression, and had
gone forth for weary and troubled years in self-
denying works, was strangely rewarded. That
overshadowing wrong, whose hideous shadow had
rested with blight and mildew on all the land,
and from which no human foresight could per-
ceive relief, was finally, wonderfully obliterated,
and the foremost peril of the nation was forever
removed.

The world saw the hand of God in these events.
Thanksgivings to Him who is over all, mingled
with the sorrows of the bereaved who sat in solitariness in every home. It was seen that the dead
had not died in vain. The purpose of Providence
was fulfilled. And therefore it is that in these
beautiful days we can honor, as we recall, those
who laid down their lives for us and for our
children.

" Once more before the summer's radiant portal
   Springs wide to welcome us, we turn to lay
   The floral wreath of May
   Upon the grave mounds of our hero dead.
   A noble land should hold their fame immortal
   Who gave their lives to keep it as a shrine
   Inviolate and pure ;
   And made it so, secure,
   Pouring their blood as sacrificial wine.
   O hero brothers ! through the victor palms
   Do ye look earthward ?   Do ye bend to greet
   The tones of human love, and find them sweet
   Rising up, broken, through transcendent psalms ?
   But, oh, beloved dead ! shall words of praise,
   Or Spring's fair blooms, suffice?
   What mean our sacred, our memorial days
   Of you whose gift of price
   To your dear land was life ?
              Nay, it is not well
   That we should rest content with words and flowers.
   Your work is done!   The task that yet is ours
   is to live nobly, striving still to make
   Righteousness rule the nation for whose sake
   Ye counted life as naught.   If in the skies
   The prayers of saints for those on earth arise,
   Ask that our work may be as nobly done,
   Our land redeemed, our rest as bravely won."

VIII

THE UPBUILDING OF THE CHURCH

"In whom each several building, fitly framed together, groweth into a holy temple in the Lord."—*Ephesians* 2 : 21.

———

AT REDEDICATION OF NORTH HAVEN CHURCH.

THE UPBUILDING OF THE CHURCH

The work of the Church in the world is a great
work. Whether we look at it as a whole, or in its
parts, it suggests magnitude, great forces, great
labor, great accomplishment. It was great in its
origin; in which the divine hand was employed.
It has been great in its progress; in which the
best talent and the choicest culture have found
field for their exercise. It will be great in its conclusion; in which varied agencies in the widest
use and over the broadest realms will be summoned to superlative activity.

In any given locality, as in a single parish, the
church of that place has a great work upon its
hands. It is a force of civilization. The Church
is anti-barbarian. Inasmuch as human nature
runs into barbaric moods, tends to chaos and old
night, readily takes on habits of brutality, sensual-
ism, vulgarness, it must be met, checked, held
back, by humanizing, civilizing processes, otherwise it would degenerate into utter barbarism.
Lawlessness and lewdness and intemperance would

play havoc with the family, with government, with education, with all social order.

But the Church is a force of *civilization*. It anchors the family among men. It inaugurates and sustains marriage. It cherishes childhood among the loves of home, and throws around youth the tender restraints of domestic affection, of filial reverence and gratitude. It stigmatizes vice, and it sustains law. Philanthropists and humanitarians, in their work for men, have found it their chief auxiliary, and have relied upon it more than upon any worldly, sumptuary or municipal agencies. A man, actuated by simply worldly, prejudicial, selfish motives, planting a town or establishing a colony, would give a lot and subscribe largely for a church. The opposite course has been tried. It was tried in a western community, and it was found that churchless, godless society soon lost even its civilization, and pushed into the most unblushing and foul vice; that property there was not worth holding; that you could not get public spirit, nor private charity, nor common decency on any such basis, and that the attempt to plant society in that way was conspicuous failure.

The Church is also a force of *education*. I would not go so far as to claim that all good teachers are Christians; although the facts on that point would startle you; but I claim that all good

Christians are teachers, and that their life and example and influence are uplifting on society, and lead out into development and activity and the growth of the best things in men. Stephen Girard tried to plant in Philadelphia a creedless college, andforbade the entrance of any minister of the gospel within its walls, and ruled out all doctrinal Christianity from its instructions. But its presidents and teachers have been Christian men, and a religious service is held on every Lord's day within its classic marble halls, and its students have come forth to be members of Christian churches. The Chritianity of Philadelphia has poured all around the stone ramparts that guard like a fortification the estate of the college, and embraced it with the principles of Christ, which are stronger than those of Mr. Girard. Christian schools and homes and literature, and the lives of Christian men and women have power on rising minds. They give thought, suggest inquiry and motives and results, set men forward in endeavors, stimulate progress and cultivation. They lay the groundwork of a broad and substantial education.

The Church is also a force of *conversion*. The example of its members has power in this direction. Their prayerful, righteous lives, their upright, daily walk, the principles which they carry into business, into politics, into social life, into domestic life, are converting principles. The child

is won to religion by the father or mother; the
merchant by his brother merchant; the neighbor
by his neighbor; the friend by friend. So the
work of conversion goes forward. The preaching
of the gospel is for this. It brings the most
important truths to men, and they are influenced
by them, and one by one they yield to them as
they ought to yield. So congregations are saved;
so communities are transformed; so the work of
the world's salvation progresses. I do not stop
now to speak of a thousand other influences which
are exerted by the church in any given place. I
throw out these three bold forms of its power as a
civilizing, educational, conversional force, and challenge for it regard in those respects. If it did
nothing else it would be the foremost institution of
society. If it did nothing else it should be permanently planted and generously sustained and successfully worked. It may be given to a man to do
many other good things; to build up a prosperous
business which shall support many people; to
beautify a city so that multitudes shall enjoy the
products of nature and the works of art that he
has gathered within its boundaries; to endow a
school or college which shall educate young men
and women from year to year for the larger duties
of life; to open a hospital which shall be free to
the sufferers in body or mind; to donate Bibles
and tracts and useful books for the daily reading

and sanctification of the people; to improve the
drainage, or the food, or the clothing, or the commerce, or the products of a region.   But there is
nothing to which he will look back with more satisfaction than to the successful planting of a useful
Christian church.   Such a church will be an
unfailing fountain of good in the community.   It
will lift up the place in good manners and morals;
it will encourage the refinements of life; it will be
an educator, it will foster schools and stimulate
teachers, and it will send out men and books and
cultivated men and women; it will exert a trans-
forming power on generation after generation, and
perpetuate a succession of Christians.   It will stand
through centuries, till the millennium; it will stand
through the millennium, aiding in the work which
will bring on that period and rejoicing throughout
those happy ages in the victories that have been
gained.   There is, therefore, no better work that a
man can do; no better way in which he can
appropriate money or effort than in behalf of a
Christian church.   He may take the broadest view
and yield himself to a sympathy with the world-
work of churches, the work which they are carrying on for the civilizing, education, conversion of
all nations, and he will be a broader and better
man for it.   He will feel in himself the broadening, elevating, inspiring influence of it.   Or he
may take the narrower view of the home work, the

work right around him; and there will be enough
in that to make him a good deal of a man if he
will fully put himself into harmony with it.   He
will not need to go to Japan to find bright minds,
nor to the Hottentots to find dull ones, nor to
China to get hold of a great work, nor to India to
find inspiration in saving men.   He can have his
hands full, and his heart full, and his brain full
within a comfortable walk from his own step-stone,
and there he can make his life powerful and eminently useful.   The trouble is not that there is not
work enough everywhere, but that we don't do it.
We let things slide along; we let our neighbors
slide along; we let the church slide along; we let
everything in the matter of Christian activity slide
along; whereas we ought to concern ourselves
with its going along and with its most successful
progress.

We ought not as Christians, here, to be satisfied
with anything less than will satisfy our brothers in
Hawaii or Constantinople: the complete elevation
and Christianization of the community.   One by
one we should bring all these people to Christ.
One by one we should have all these homes Christian homes.   The work on our hands is great and
inviting and stimulating.

For this work there is need of *union*.   The
membership of a church should be one.   It should
stand together and work together in this cause;

for it is its cause and the cause of its Master. One of the old cities of Greece was built without walls. It stood on the open plain, defenceless. Other rival cities had their strong and elaborate defences, in ramparts and towers and moats and gates of brass. When one of its great citizens was asked why his city was built in that unprotected manner, he replied, "The concord of its citizens is the defence of the city." The united hearts of its people were its granite walls. Their lofty love was its impregnable towers. Had hostile foe approached, every Lacedæmonian body would have stood in the solid array for its protection. Such a city could not be taken. Such a city was full of strength. It was all power.

We want the Lacedæmonian spirit in the Church. Union, the union of love, the union of Christian kindness, of generous straightforwardness with one another, the union that will bring us into the ranks with the ardent quickstep of volunteers, will make work easy and pleasant and successful. There is enthusiasm in the united shout: that is the voice of victory. There is momentum in the movement of the whole body, the grand progress of the tidal wave which bears everything before it. There is strength in numbers, in the presence of the whole, in the feeling that there are no laggards, that we move together. The building that is fitly framed together groweth into a temple. Beams, joists,

rafters, though of various wood, grown on different mountainsides, cut and prepared by different
hands, if adjusted to each other and made to fit
by the plans of the architect, and solidly united by
tenons and mortices, will make a firm and durable
structure. The church may be made up of different individuals, — men of culture and men of
coarseness, some with learning and some without
it, some with the experience and ripeness of age,
and others with the freshness and rawness of
youth, some with ability, and others with decided
inability; but each one has his place, and when
in it he is of decided value, and contributes to the
strength and beauty and usefulness of the organization. The broad beam, the sleeper, the slender
joist and rafter, the little pin that holds them together, contribute to the solidity and grace and
durability and worth of the majestic temple. The
union of all the parts is essential to the growth of
the structure.

This union must be " in Christ," " in whom each
building, several fitly framed together, groweth into
a holy temple in the Lord." The chief corner-stone
is Jesus Christ. All our work must be in him and
upon him. We must be one in him. Our love for
one another must be sanctified by our greater love
for him. Our service must spring from our joy in
him and our gratitude to him. Christ must be the
inspiration of our song; the motive for our labor;

the object of our prayer; the source of our happiness; the comfort of our suffering. We must begin with him and end in him. Real concord will come to any church through the union of all in Christ. The more each one is bound to the Saviour, the more will each one be bound to all the others. "In him" each stone and timber of the temple is to be fitly framed, and then it will grow into a holy temple. The strength of the Church is in its Head. Numbers cannot take the place of One. Wealth cannot make up for Him. Power cannot fill his place. Influence cannot. Young men are not sufficient. Learned men would not avail without Him. You may build on social influence, on riches, on the culture of the few or the power of the many, on the multitude of the young, on worldly maxims, on philosophy; but the true architecture is of Christ. He must be the foundation-stone, and the manifold hearts of Christians that make up the rising temple must be cemented in love to Him. Here is strength and durability and beauty as well. Christ is the true Lord.

On an old Swiss coin was the device, a stalwart soldier leaning on a mighty sword, with the inscription, "*Deus providebit.*" The strong soldier and the tempered blade! her sturdy sons and their true weapons! not these are the real strength of Switzerland. Her granite mountains rise grand-

ly around and her puissant soldiers can defend
every pass. But not in these is the glory and
strength of the republic. God will take care!
The strength of the hills is his. The might of the
bold soldiery comes from Omnipotence. " A
mighty fortress is our God." " God is the refuge
of his saints." We build on Christ. He is our
corner-stone. In him alone is strength and salvation. The Church is strong because its Head is
strong. We overcome in his might. The soldier
is well: we must have him. And the true sword
of tempered steel: we must have that. But *Deus
providebit*. Christ is more. He is all. Without
him all else were vain. With him all else will
prosper. In all our work let us put him foremost.
Let the love we bear to Christ be first. For his
sake let us labor; for his sake win others to him.
There is no holy temple unless he is its foundation. There is no saved world unless he is its
Saviour. There are no burdens lifted unless the
Burden-bearer takes them.

" Lazarus lies unfed and fainting—Peter sinks beneath the
        wave ;
Loving Mary lingers sadly near the Saviour's guarded grave ;
Blind Bartimeus, by the wayside, begs his bread disconsolate ;
For the moving of the waters, at the pool the suffering wait;
In the wilderness the lepers wander, outcast, in their pain;
Paul and Silas, in the prison, bear the fetter and the chain;
Mary Magdalene is weeping, friendless in her sin and shame ;
But their burdens all were lifted when the Burden-bearer
        came."

This church in entering anew upon Christian
work within its home field is entering upon no
untried or novel enterprise. We know that true
labor here yields harvest. We have a fivefold
work :

First, in respect to our membership. There
are members of this church who are not with
us, who do not even worship with us, who have
lost their place and, I do not doubt, have lost their
comfort and Christian joy. Let us bring the wanderers back to the Lord and to us. There are
those here who should become members with us.
Let us show them that we are their brethren and
give them the right hand of affectionate fellowship.

Secondly, in respect to our children, that they
may be all taught of God and may be gathered
with us.

Thirdly, in respect to the poor and the sick,
that we may kindly administer to them in the
Master's name and cheer them in their loneliness
and pain.

Fourthly, in respect to the multitude who have
no church home, attend on no public worship,
care not for these things nor for their souls. Let
us be God's missionaries to them and by the love
that moves our brethren in China and Japan and
Micronesia seek the salvation of these who are at
our own doors.

Fifthly, in respect to strangers, those who have

come to this place from other places, who have
left dear friends and beloved churches and pleasant associations and settled by our side. Let us
make them feel that here, too, they are among
friends who will love them, who will gladly do
them service, who will help them on the way to
the other shore. Let us make our pleasant places
pleasant places for them, so that they shall not
regret that they have cast anchor in this haven:
so that here they shall see the Lord in his followers and with them experience the joy of his
presence.

This is our fivefold work. Into it we must put
the resolution to do it, zeal to crowd it forward,
energy as in any business, and determination to be
thorough in it and to actually accomplish it.
Back of it we must put our tender, earnest, believing prayer, sensible that not our efforts nor our
union can avail to build up the church or to save
souls without the help of God; that it is not by
human might nor power, but by the Spirit of God,
that these services of ours can be made effective.
Then will the blessing come, full-flooded, pouring
from the boundless Source, and filling all our
hearts. May God hasten it and glorify his
name!

The apostle, in this figure, compares the Church
to a temple; its growth to the upbuilding of a
large and costly structure. Whether this epistle

is correctly inscribed to the Ephesians or not,
those to whom he wrote were familiar with the
architectural glories of Greece. The magnificent
temples, whose stately and beautiful proportions
rose high over all other works, were the pride and
crown of the rival and regal cities in which
flourished and bloomed in such perfect maturity
the high art of the ancient world.

But there was no temple like that at Ephesus.
The glories of Athens and the splendors of Corinth
could not equal it. It was one of the wonders of
the world. The sun in all his course looked down
on nothing so magnificent. Its fame filled the
nations and men from foreign lands sought it with
enthusiasm. It stood at the head of the harbor
and the sheen of its white walls glistened upon the
sea. It was built in the beautiful Ionic style whose
graceful forms and proportions are so grateful to
the genius of the Asiatic Greek. Its immense
foundations were carefully laid. It was designed
by the most accomplished architects. It was 425
feet in length and 220 in breadth. It had 127
columns of choicest marble and each of them was
the gift of a king. All the Greek cities of Asia
contributed to its erection. A rich foreign king
gave his munificent donation. Its doors were of
cypress wood. Its roof was of cedar. Its staircase was made of the wood of a single vine from
Cyprus. The ladies of Ephesus gave their jewelry

toward its erection. The finest pictures and statues of the artists adorned it. It was the glory of Ephesus.

Alexander offered to give the spoils of a campaign to it if only his name might be inscribed upon the temple, but it was not permitted. No name could add to its peerless glory. No wealth could place a human name upon its divine walls. It contained within its vaults gems and jewels and gold greater than the wealth of many kings. A thousand years were spent in its erection and adornment.

But the apostle saw a diviner Temple. Its foundations were laid by no human hands. God was its Architect. It covered the world with its magnificent proportions. Its fame was to go out among the principalities and powers of other worlds. All lands were to contribute to it. Kings were to be its patrons and queens its benefactors. The songs within it were to be in all the tongues of men. Prayer should ascend unceasingly from its altars. It would be the glory and joy of the whole earth. Above all it would be the habitation of God. The Divine Spirit would dwell within it.

My brethren: We are the living stones of this temple. Within us dwells the Holy Spirit. Are we the fit habitation of such a guest? Do we cherish his presence? Do we honor him in all our thoughts and plans? Is our daily life pleasing to him? Are our words and acts, our business, our ambitions, our pleasures, honorable to him?

For the upbuilding of this temple, in our day, let us unweariedly labor! Our names, the humblest name among us, may go upon its walls. In its eternal wealth we may all freely share.

IX

THE POWER OF THE CHURCH

"Ye shall receive power, when the Holy Ghost is come upon you: and ye shall be my witnesses both in Jerusalem, and in all Judæa and Samaria, and unto the uttermost part of the earth."—*Acts* 1 : 8.

AT QUARTER-CENTURY ANNIVERSARY.

Rival forces, in ceaseless antagonism, are struggling for the mastery of the world. In manifold
methods and with varying fortunes, through the
ages, under the control of divine Providence, the
conflict proceeds. It proceeds, at one period,
through the wrestling of opposing thought; and
at another period through the clash of opposing
arms; now by the setting up of institutions which
are to live and grow old and control the civilization of states; and then through the overthrow of
prerogative and dynasty and social order. It
proceeds, at one era, under the leadership of a
single imperial mind, marshaling other minds in
obedience to its genius; and at another era by the
simultaneous movement of whole masses, swayed
by a common principle and enforcing a common
purpose; now by revolutions that seem to receive
their impetuosity from below; and then by regen-
erations which are characterized by their divine
origin, and which carry blessings, wherever they
are effective, to mankind. Great periods in his-

tory are marked by the rise and success of domi-
nating systems, which, for the time, move the
world; by the life and deeds of great men whose
conquering footsteps reverberate around the globe;
by the power and intensity of ideas which project
themselves into the life, the language, the literature, the whole rational being, of peoples. Who
shall rule the world? What shall be supreme?
These are the questions, not of this day only, but
of all time. Power is what men want. To con-
quer the world has been the supreme ambition.
The place of power—that is the place where
crowns are. Palaces hold it; courts surround it;
honors wait on it; greatest things are tributary to
it. Milton is the secretary of Cromwell; the
mightier serves the mighty! Kings are not those
only who mount the world's thrones. The royalest
kingship is that of mind. The King of kings rules
by moral power. He holds physical forces in his
omnipotent hand, so that he who made all worlds
could destroy all worlds; but his divinest regality
is his lordship of minds that are free.

Christ taught his disciples that they were in the
world to overcome the world; that his kingdom,
which they were to advance, was a conquering
kingdom; and that power would be given to
them to make it successful to the uttermost part
of the earth. The text indicates the substance of
their power, the source from which it was to be

derived, and the sphere in which it was to be exercised.

In its SUBSTANCE it is whatever efficiency was necessary for their success. It included, in the apostolic era, control over natural laws and interference with their normal working, the mighty power of miracles, as though even the divine prerogatives were transferred to them; but it included, also, the wide range of influence which belongs to all eras, by which man controls his fellow man, the power of earnest, vigorous, intelligent mind over all other minds in arresting attention, swaying affections, and even forcing the unforced will.

In its source it is divine; either the power of the Holy Ghost being directly imparted to the disciples, or giving extraordinary efficiency to their own capabilities by his influence upon them, so that it might be truly said that their success is not by might, nor by power, but by the Spirit of the Lord.

In its SPHERE it is world-wide, encompassing the uttermost parts of the earth, and solving the redemption of the race. It is a power wrought in the home field, wrought in the foreign field as well, both in Jerusalem, and in all Judæa, and in Samaria, and unto the uttermost part of the earth.

My subject is: *The Power of the Church to take Possession of the World.*

And I wish to make this subject practical by insisting that it is the duty of Christians to use this

power, now. The time is upon us when the world
should be taken for Christ. The prayer, " Thy
kingdom come," instead of referring in a slow and
general way to some remote millennium, whose
golden light no magnifying glass is powerful
enough yet to discover, should be offered with the
expectation of its immediate answering.

The promises, which embrace the subjection of
all kingdoms and powers to the one Lord of all,
should be interpreted as capable of fulfilment in
the midst of the marvels that are now transpiring.

We have a historical demonstration of what can
be done in the *early spread of Christianity*. The
apostles and early Christians regarded the power
which they received as power to be used and to
be made effective. They welcomed the bestowal
of the Holy Spirit because his aid, his divine
working in them, was essential to their success
as the promulgators of the gospel. Securing this
promised and blessed agency they entered vigor-
ously and victoriously upon the conquest of the
world. Never were the obstacles greater. Never
was opposition more firmly entrenched. Judaism,
hoary with age, defiant in its enmity, stood on the
one hand. Heathenism, dominant and strong, and
holding the centers of learning and power, stood
on the other hand. Both were leagued against
Christianity. Bigotry, philosophy, power; Jerusalem, Athens, Rome; all were to be met, all were

to be mastered. The early Christians did not
falter. With a sublime courage, with a genuine
enthusiasm, with a peerless patience, with an
undoubting confidence, through perils of the most
formidable character, at the loss of all things but
their own fidelity, they carried their cause forward.
They carried it forward until it was the foremost
force in the world; until in Jerusalem it was
greater than Judaism; until in Athens Christ was
greater than Plato; until in Rome the mighty
emperor wore above his crown a cross. They
suffered, but the cause prospered. They endured
martyrdom, but their principles were crowned.
Their death gave new life to the gospel. It held
on its conquering way and the world yielded to
its mastery. This wonderful success of the first
Christian ages stands out in the forefront of
history as a demonstration of the power of the
Church to take possession of the world; to retake
the world. That which was done, may again be
done. That which was done, must again be done.
We have the same cause; we have the same glorious Leader; we need only the same energizing
Spirit, only the same grace of Christ, only the
same indwelling and outgoing word of God; the
three onlys of the great historian.

We have also the repeated demonstration of
what can be done by the energizing *power of the
Holy Spirit* in the disciples. This was seen at

first; it has been repeatedly seen in subsequent
experience. Christ taught his apostles that it was
expedient for them that he should go away, for if
he did not depart the Comforter would not come
to them. When the Spirit came, the apostles
became new men. A transformation, like a new
birth, passed upon them. They rose to a grander
stature, and they undertook a wider work. Peter,
in the very presence of Christ, denied him. When
the Spirit came he was the bold champion of his
Master everywhere. When the Spirit came, power
came. And then these few and feeble disciples
coped successfully with every form of opposition.
Not only did the Spirit work in them to give them
personal power, but he worked with the word they
uttered to give it power wherever it went, so that
it was indeed the word of God, quick and powerful, overcoming and renewing. The pentecostal
seasons, when thousands yielded to the word of
one; the great revivals, which have come after
great declensions, breaking up worldliness and
indifference and formality, giving reality to this
life and solemn meaning to the life to come,
awakening interest and earnestness and profound
anxiety as to the soul and its readiness to stand
face to face with God, clothing the word of God
with the deepest significance, and bringing great
multitudes to seek salvation as the one thing needful, testify to this power of the Spirit. It may be

simultaneously, everywhere put forth. We who labor in this land, our honored brethren in older lands, our sons and daughters who have gone with the Word to newest lands, all may feel his reviving, sanctifying power, may see his renewing, saving power, at one time, bringing multitudes to Christ, giving birth to nations in a day, and making the world's conquest complete. What we have witnessed, the marvelous events that are already recorded of the work of the Holy Spirit on individual minds, on masses of men, on communities, on whole peoples, predict the rapid conversion of the world when the time shall come for the full putting forth of his wonderful energy. Then the work shall go forward as in a geometrical ratio. One circle of holy influence shall widen until it shall sweep within the circumference of another, and these again shall roll within the orbits of others still, and so broadening and revolving they shall encompass the globe with their luminous lines.

On this divine aid the Church can rely in its work of making conquest of the world. Christians are possessors of this gift of grace. The Holy Spirit is promised to them. He comes in the place of Christ. He comes to be the Leader of Christ's own. What Christ would do were he with us in his personal presence, the Spirit will now do for us. And so soon as we learn to rely on him

and cooperate with him, great and marvelous results may be expected,—nothing less than the
possession of the world for its Lord.

It has fallen to my lot of late to spend several
communion Sabbaths with the church with which
I was first connected in my native city, and to
administer to it the sacrament of the Supper. It is
a large church, of over 400 members, embracing a
great deal of mental ability, of social and worldly
strength, and of spiritual resource. There are
some men in it of remarkable talent. As I was
standing by the communion table, on the first Sabbath of the year, looking over that great and intelligent body of Christians as they passed out of the
beautiful church, the oldest officer of the church,
who was standing by me, remarked: "There is
power here." Yes; that remark was full of suggestion: power enough there to take and hold
that city for Christ. And it belongs to those
Christians, with their brethren of other denomina-
tions, to do it.

It is reported by a Methodist brother of some
Unitarian ministers who looked on at a recent camp-
meeting, that they were heard to say, "If we only
had this power of faith, we could take the world."
They recognized the divine mastery of a principle
in the glowing hearts around them which should
subdue the world.

A great deal of important *preliminary work* has

already been accomplished toward this conquest and in recognition of its approach. I refer briefly to a few symbols of it. The churches which are builded for Christian worship sustain an analogous relation in this conquest to that which fortresses do to the military occupation of a country. They stand as the fortifications of truth, as the magazines of influence, as the citadels of power. They are planted on the most conspicuous and accessible sites. They are often made very attractive and impressive in their size, proportions and adornments. Christian architecture, in the vast and imposing cathedrals, in the beautiful and homelike churches, on which hard earnings and regal wealth have been expended, providing rendezvous and attractive accessories of worship and accustoming the people to the idea of Christ's Lordship, has done much to prepare the way for, and to familiarize the mind with, the Christian conquest of the world.

So of the public, secular *recognition of religion.* The practice, in Christian states, of associating the ministers of religion with important events, as by their public prayers at the organization of important deliberative assemblies, at the beginning of great national works, of social or industrial or educational institutions, accustoms the people to the recognition of God, and carries his claims to their attention into the daily and significant affairs of

11

life. So is he acknowledged as Lord. A step
further, is the world's possession by him.

And more important is the authority given to
the Bible. It is recognized as a sacred book. Its
words, sounding down all the centuries, freighted
with the joys and griefs and exultant hopes and
victories of saints through past millenniums, vocal
even with the thoughts of angels, and full of the
expression of Christ himself, are accepted as the
Word of God. The Bible is the stronghold of
Christianity. The churches could not maintain
themselves without it. Infidelity, spiritism, every
antagonist system, smites at the Bible; scoffs at
this divine Word; would weaken, would gladly destroy its authority. It stands, the same old Bible,
with the memory of the dead in it; with the warm
loves of childhood in it; with the woe of our trials
reverberating in its melancholy experiences; and
the joys of our better days ringing in its psalms
and prophecies like chimes of musical bells above
the lower life, stands. It is always God's Word.
The better life of the people is in it. On it are
sworn the oaths which make our courts of justice
our palladiums. The magistrate has power because the Bible is. The nation has its foundation
on this book which is laid in the corner-stones of
its temples and its capitals. Its words are like
choice music which we cannot forget; its promises
are like faces that ever beam on us in their remem-

bered expression; it is like a life within our life,
warming and refreshing and invigorating us.

The hold of the Bible on the popular mind is a
most auspicious signal of the conquest of the
world by the Church. It has prepared the way
for all labor. It is as though the fortresses of the
country to be gained were already carried.

The power of the Church over the world may
be made efficient by manifold methods. It belongs to it to exercise power over *popular thought*.
The learning of the world is largely within the
Church. Science finds its most earnest students
among those who believe in Him who made all
things. The wide and captivating fields of literature are enthusiastically cultivated by those who
reverence the revelation of God. To our great
scholars, to our cultured penmen, and our accomplished orators and our devout scientists, is committed the task of giving the world correct ideas
and of molding public opinion. It is for them to
demonstrate the true science and to advance the
wise theory of life and to chasten the imagination.
On all subjects which summon forth the popular
thought they are to be leaders; on the one hand
assailing and controverting specious and false
notions, and on the other advocating and establishing safe and sound theories, whether within the
domain of this life, or related to the life unseen
and eternal.

It belongs to it also to possess an *educational power* on the rising and advancing mind. Christians have seen the importance of this force in the world, and, wise in their day, they have laid the endowment of schools by the endowment of churches, and furnished books as they have furnished sermons for the training of minds that are advancing into influence and control. This power must not be lost; it must rather be nurtured and augmented. Not by the secularizing of our schools and universities are we to fulfill our mission in our day; rather by the more perfect Christianizing of them. Let earnest Christian scholars stand at the head of them, and let the Bible be an undoubted authority within them. I remember once to have heard, at the morning worship in Christ Church College, at Oxford, a college which was founded by Cardinal Wolsey, that most tender and sublime anthem, " I will arise and go unto my Father," subduingly rendered by accomplished singers, with a grand organ accompaniment, leading, as it would seem, truant, lost souls back to their Father. And I felt that if Christ's precious words were day by day so sounding through those ancient halls of learning, where, too, the memory of some of Christ's most faithful witnesses ever lives, that Oxford, however perverted, must be held back, brought back, to Christ. Not the old universities only and old communities must be

educated for Christ; but especially must rising
communities and the new institutions be taught
and held for him.

It belongs to the Church also to retain power in
social and national life; in social life, making
Christian principles dominant, and so regulating
the morals and manners of the people; in political life, holding, if nothing more, the balance of
power in such way as to keep good men in official
station, and to secure integrity and uprightness in
civil affairs. Franklin, writing, at a critical era,
from Philadelphia to his brother in Boston, spoke
of the prayers of Christians in New England as
" giving a vast balance in favor" of what he and
they deemed to be the right side. These prayers
were simultaneous with the assembling of a strong
land and naval force to act for the same purpose
as the prayers.

This power of the Church may also be efficiently
used in *direct efforts to save* men. For this, indeed, is the Church. Its object is to save the
world. The work of individual Christians should
be to secure the salvation of others, of the lost
ones, of all the lost; like the Lord, not willing
that any should perish, but that all should come
to repentance. Knowing the grace of Christ, it is
for them to carry that grace to those for whom
he died, even as he died for them. Here, in
fact, is the divinest power of the Church; here is

the work which lifts them closest to the side of
Christ.

Some statements have been made in respect to
the rapidity with which the world can be taken by
this work of conversion. It has been stated that
in this land, where one seventh of the population
are Christians, if each one of these should, under
God, bring six persons to Christ during the next
year, at the end of the year the land would be
wholly converted. Also, that if one Christian
should lead one soul to Christ in a year, the two,
two more in the second year, and so on in this
ratio, before the end of a single lifetime the whole
world would be converted. Further, that if five
hundred thousand should each work effectively for
one soul yearly, and so on, in thirteen years the
world would be saved.

Such results as these, by the divine blessing,
are not too much to expect. They are within the
compass of a faithful Church. The experience of
the faithful, earnest Church warrants their fulfilment.

Ah, the faithful, earnest Church !

A distinguished politician, who was accustomed
to carry elections, who had been the governor of
his state and for many years her senator in congress, whose fiery, impetuous eloquence swayed
the masses and bore down opposition, once
chanced to attend the meeting of a Bible society.

A deplorable account was given of Bible destitu-
tion. The old senator heard the lifeless narrative
and sprang to the floor, requesting to be heard.
In bold language he charged upon the brethren
that they were not in earnest. Said he, " In the
great contest for the election of Harrison, we
Whig members of Congress gave our whole
salaries to carry that election. We thought the
salvation of the country depended upon it. If you
want to carry on this work, and really mean that
every man shall have the Bible, you must go to
work and give every man the Bible." The assembly was electrified ; the senator was at once made
president of the society, and it was not again reported that a single family in that county was
without the Bible. The earnest church can save
the world.

In one of the old libraries of Philadelphia, I
have read a foreign work on " The Glorious Recovery by the Vaudois of their Valleys," by Henri
Arnaud, their pastor and commander. Nearly
two centuries ago the Duke of Savoy undertook to
banish them from their wild valleys where they
had long maintained their simple and faithful
worship. They clung to their altars and their
homes and their magnificent mountains. Fourteen thousand of this devoted people were thrown
into prison. Three thousand only survived, and
they went out from their old abodes with broken

hearts. homeless, solitary wanderers. They took
refuge in Switzerland and Germany; but they
were not at home. Their hearts were over the
mountains, and the verdant valleys lay green in
their longing thought. The songs of the wild torrents rang in their regretful memories, and no
music could charm them away. The snow-clad
summits, brilliant in golden sunlight, rose white
and pure to their open-eyed vision. The starry
heavens which bent and glowed and smiled above
Lucerne and St. Martin and Perouse were reflected
in their tearful eyes, as in the lakes that lay beneath them. The swift streams that burst coldly
from the blue glaciers rushed not more impetu-
ously forward than did their hearts go bounding
back. Every grave of the sweet valleys drew them,
every home called for them, every footpath on the
steep mountainside summoned them; voices of
the air and of the woods, and of the mountain
flowers, voices of kindred, and of passionate love,
and of true religion whispered and wailed and
cried for their return.

The Vaudois would go. Three times, against
desperate odds, they made the attempt. Twice
they were turned back in utter defeat. The third
time they were successful. Eight hundred armed
men, their solitary hope, crossed Lake Geneva and
began the passage of the Alps to recover their
lost, loved valleys. Thousands of troops and all

the inhabitants of the land opposed them. Over
the mountains, across the swift streams, through
the valleys, in prayer, in arms, with one solemn
purpose, with one masterful love, they pushed
right on. Every day was one of toil. Every day
was one of battle. Sometimes their way was
through the trackless snow. It was reddened with
their blood. They passed over precipices where no
foe dared to follow. Their number grew less as
their valleys drew near. At length they entered
them. With thanks but not with peace their feet
stood again upon the dear soil. Hostile troops in
overwhelming numbers were moved against them.
Driven from one valley and then from another,
they seized and fortified the towering Balsi, a
mighty pinnacle of rock, and there kept up their
tireless defence through the long-months of winter.

When extermination seemed inevitable, they
fled, but still kept sight, on the mountains, of their
own valleys. Finally the offer of peace came, and
they recovered their valleys. Liberty of conscience
was guaranteed. The gospel was again preached.
These faithful witnesses for the truth were kept for
the work of our day.

Such faith and love and undying earnestness
recovered the valleys of Piedmont. Such faith
and love and holy earnestness would recover the
world. Can we doubt it?

To a weak faith the work seems immense, per-

haps impossible. But with our God all things are
possible. A few years ago I stood here, the citizen of a land cursed beyond the power of expression by a system of human bondage, against which
I bore earnest testimony, but for deliverance from
which I saw no possibility. But deliverance came.
It came in the throes and agonies of protracted
war, protracted till we could learn well the terrible
lesson of our crime and till blows had fallen for
every bondman's lash, and blood of freemen had
answered for the blood of slaves. A new nation,
purged by fire, tried by the ordeal of battle, took
its place in history. God gave the nation a new
birth. In a few years was effected the reorganiza-
tion of state and society.

A few months ago the Papal power ruled in
Rome, upheld by the support of an empire which
stood at the head of the world. The prestige of
French power was upon all the nations. In a
fatal hour the perjured emperor, in the folly of a
self-confidence which proved his ruin, threw
down the gauntlet before a Protestant kingdom,
invoking the arbitrament of battle. The land of
Luther resented the imperial insult and rose unit-
edly in arms. The spiked helmets of the German warriors crossed the Rhine and bristled in the
gardens of the Tuileries. The armies, the power,
the prestige of France, were overthrown; the German empire, great and glorious, rose to the first

rank among the nations. It is difficult to com-
prehend the magnitude of this revolution. Already Rome has passed into other hands, and the
children of the Vaudois proclaim the gospel of the
valleys in its churches. Already another reformation is sweeping through Germany. A Protestant
power stands at the head of the world. All this
predicts great changes yet to be. All this demonstrates the possibility of changes which may revo-
lutionize the world, and give the kingdom to the
Son of God. As in a day there may be the up-
heaval of institutions, powers, peoples, whole races
of mankind. As in a day superstitions, idolatries,
old religions, may be subverted and pass into forgetfulness. As in a day the people of the Most
High may come to rule the world.

Surely, what we have seen in our own time may
take away our unbelief, and give us confidence in
Him who rules the world in the interest of his
truth and of his people.

TWENTY-FIVE YEARS AGO TO-DAY, at this very
hour, it fell to my lot to receive ordination as the
minister of this church. And when lately invited
by your honored pastor to stand once more in the
old place and to speak to you as long ago, it
seemed fit and pleasant that I should select this
sacred hour, so full of undying memories, so suggestive to us all. That day of ordination was a
day of wondrous beauty : it heralded a work

which went forward for more than fourteen years.
Of the beloved ministers who took part in the in-
teresting services, only two survive, one of whom
is my neighbor still, in Philadelphia, and one of
whom is your neighbor and fellow citizen.   Of the
officers and members of the church at that time,
the majority, I suppose, are no longer here.

Some things remain.   The same skies bend over
you with their blazing constellations.   The same
hills rise on this landscape of charming beauty.
The same tides ebb and flow in the river and the
sea.   This Bible changes not.   The same old, old
story sounds on with its unchanging love.   Christ
is the same yesterday and to-day and forever.   The
Holy Spirit, whose work we often saw wrought
with wondrous power, still dwells among us and
still wins all our hearts to repentance and faith.

But during this quarter of a century there have
been wonderful changes.   Many who were with us
and were dear to us have exchanged this world for
heaven, and all their experience is new.   I recall
the blessed peace of dying ones, their victory of
faith, their delightful foresight of the glorious
land.

I have referred to the change that has passed
over our land, for the fulfilment of our liberty, in
which you also bore a part on land and sea, and
for which you gave your quota of heroes; also to
some changes in older lands.   Sweeping a wider

field, through this quarter-century, we see so much accomplished, so many evolutions wrought, that a new world stands before us.   And greater marvels shall transpire. God's divine plans are to move on, and revolutions are to transform the world.   In His work, let us, my friends, old and new, be on the right side, which is, in the long run, the winning side. " He always wins who sides with God." Let us, as faithful to the Lord, be among the foremost who shall take possession of the world and win its crowns for Christ.

X

OUR FOREFATHERS

" We have heard with our ears,
   O God, our fathers have told us,
   What work thou didst in their days, in the days of old.
   Thou didst drive out the nations with thy hand, and
      plantedst them in ;
   Thou didst afflict the peoples, and didst spread them
      abroad.
   For they gat not the land in possession by their own
      sword,
   Neither did their own arm save them :
   But thy right hand, and thine arm, and the light of thy
      countenance,
   Because thou hadst a favour unto them."

Psalms 44 : 1–3.

———

NEW HAVEN AND PHILADELPHIA.

OUR FOREFATHERS

I am to speak to you to-day of *the Forefathers of New England.*

It is something to have forefathers who are worthy of our commemoration, of whom we can speak with pride and affectionate remembrance. Other peoples trace back their lineage to a base root, to a supine and savage ancestry. Rome, Sparta, the ancient states, as a disguise for the meanness of their origin, claimed to have sprung from the gods, the gods having no existence save in fancy and in fable. The modern empires, France, Russia, Austria, and their rivals, have struggled up to their eminences from barbaric beginnings, and if their people were to celebrate the founding of their dynasties, they would look back into the gloom and degradation of ancient savageness.

It is our fortune, as the people of New England, to have as the fathers and founders of our commonwealths men of condition and of character; men learned, religious, puissant, heroic; men who could look difficulties and dangers in the face without flinching; men who, like seers, scanned

the future and acted in view of what was to come;
men who, by their courtly manners, their scholarly
tastes, their muscular strength and their nervous
faith, would have graced any state in its most
polished period.   One can hardly help feeling, in
tracing the history of our beginning, in limning
the early actors on our soil, that, with all our
boasted progress, it would be difficult, in many
most essential qualities, to match them by their
successors of any generation so far.   The stalwart and soldierly persons of our forefathers were
only representatives of their sturdy and masculine
minds.   They loom forth in history with a grandeur of character and a strength of achievement
which it were hard to parallel from their posterity.

Two hundred and thirty-nine years ago a vessel
of one hundred and eighty tons' burden rode at
anchor off Cape Cod.   Its destination was orig-
inally many leagues farther southward; but by
stress of weather, or through the ignorance or
malice of its master, it was providentially brought
to the white coasts of New England.   On the 21st
day of December, 1620, a landing was made on
Plymouth Rock, and it was decided that there the
Puritan colonization of the continent should com-
mence.   Those words, "Mayflower," "Plymouth
Rock," "the 21st of December," have become historic and memorable.   That humble landing was

the beginning of a people now numbered by millions and characterized for their intelligence, freedom, enterprise, learning, religion, manhood, benevolence. That date was the birthday of New England, whose homes and schools and churches and states are not only honored by its own sons, but are commended by strangers as well.

Let us look back a little from this point; let us retrace the track of the *Mayflower* and land on the Old World from which it sailed, that we may see what it was that drove this white-winged vessel, like a shivering sea-bird in the wintry gale, upon the stormy capes of New England. It was the work that was going on in Old England that led to the founding of the New England. That sea-girt island was then swept by storms wilder than those that dashed the surges of the deep in thunder upon its rocky promontories. The reformation was undergoing a new reform. The Church of England was getting an investigation such as the Church of Rome had had. Schooled for centuries by the use of the Bible in the vernacular tongue and by liberty to think and act for itself, the British mind was ready to carry out to legitimate conclusions the principles that had been enunciated by the Reformers and that commended themselves to the sound sense of the thoughtful people. The lessons which Episcopacy had given in its withdrawal from Papacy and in its

own separate establishment, were those which
were put into practice by an intelligent and powerful minority of the Church of England. In
this minority were nobles of the land, were learned
and salaried clergymen and even bishops of the
Church. They had discernment to see that
the Church of England was but half reformed,
and that the ideas which were fostered by many of
its observances were drifting the nation back into
the embrace of Rome. To us, the things which
disturbed and distracted the nation may seem
trivial. The giving the ring in marriage, the sign-
ing of the cross in baptism, the kneeling in par-
taking of the eucharist, the wearing of the sacer-
dotal robes, have not the meaning and the tendency now that they had then.

In those times they were significant emblems of
Romish influence and authority, they were the
links that held the Church to a false system, they
were the small signs which pointed to great principles. Later in history it was a little matter
which apparently brought on the clash of arms
between this and the mother country, an insignificant tax which the country could have paid
without feeling it. But that tax stood as the sign
of principles back of it which were vital and
important, and for which the Revolution was
carried through at immense expenditures. So
when Hooper, Bishop of Gloucester, determined

to refuse the Episcopate rather than to wear the Episcopal robes, he was not standing for a mere form, he was not refusing an insignificant habit merely. To him those robes were the badges of Rome, and if he had put them on he would have worn the livery of the mother of abominations. I need not illustrate this further.

Puritanism was the assertion of freedom from Popery. It was the maintenance of Christianity against the Church. It was the return to the Bible from the priests, to Christ from his false vicar. Non-conformity was Puritanism put into practice. Prelates, distinguished ministers, the most gifted and devoted in the English Church, in many cases, refused to conform to the demands of the state upon them for the strict observance of ecclesiastical practices which they deemed wrong. They asserted their liberty. They met the tyranny of their rulers with the firmness of principle and faith. They stood for their rights as British men. They were Christian freemen, and the iron rule of Tudor or Stuart could not make them swerve. Ejection from high and pleasant places, persecution to torture and to death, perpetual exile from home and native land, had no terrors to them compared with treachery to conscience and to God.

The contest went on until, in the language of New England's latest historian, "The law of England declared England to be uninhabitable by non-conformists." Separatism, the withdrawing from the state church and the observance of independent worship, followed. Worse and worse grew the times, more gloomy became the prospect, the alternative was persecution and death at home or exile abroad. Grave and intelligent men were planning for a foreign residence in some land where they could in peace enjoy their belief and their worship, and erect a commonwealth which should secure to them the privileges now denied in their native land.

Then commenced the exodus of our forefathers from old England. It was a great thing for them to leave such a country. There were the strong-built churches and the stately cathedrals in which they had worshiped. There were the fair homes over which trailed the rose and the ivy, and the hedge-fenced fields lying like gardens around them. There were the schools and the venerable universities in which they had studied. There were the great treasures which art and commerce and British arms and industry had accumulated in the ancient kingdom. There were the graves of their fathers and their near kindred, of kings and good men and martyrs, whom they revered. There were the friends whom they had cherished, few of whom could go with them. There was the country they loved, whose history was dear to

them, for which they had done battle, and for
which they would willingly die, and which they
would continue to call *home* wherever they should
go. But they left all behind them. In small
companies, in disguises, by artifice, through personal daring they fled from the tyranny of the
English Church and state to lands where they
could worship God in freedom. Many of them
went to Holland, which after a long and terrible
struggle had driven the Spanish tyrants from its
territory, and now gave the English Pilgrims a
cordial Dutch welcome. To that land our forefathers first went.

A congregation that had worshiped at Scrooby
in Nottinghamshire was the honored mother of
us all. Unwilling to bear the intolerable oppression of the times, its members in 1607 decided to
pass over to Holland. Against many difficulties
they at length succeeded. There went with them
their pastor, Richard Clifton, who had been an
honored rector in the English Church, and their
teacher, John Robinson, who was a man of eminent learning, virtue and wisdom, and whose
ability as a scholar and a logician attracted much
notice among the polemics of Holland. To their
company belonged also William Brewster, who
had before visited the Low Countries as an attend-
ant of the English ambassador. The exiled flock
was first folded at Amsterdam. That opulent city

was then a great commercial emporium. Palaces
lined its canals, which flowed through lines of
overshadowing trees, and on which rode ships
laden with the wealth of a world-wide traffic. In
its streets and thronged marts were sailors and
merchants with the costume and language of many
lands.

All was new to our Puritan forefathers. They
were strangers in a strange land, the tongue of
whose people was foreign to them, as were also
their manners and attire. They applied themselves lustily to labor for a livelihood, and in a
few months removed to Leyden, forty miles from
Amsterdam. That was the city which had endured so terrible a siege in the Spanish War, when
famine, pestilence and despair swept away its
determined citizens. But more than a generation
had passed since that, and 70,000 people now
inhabited it. In quietness and with the esteem of
the people our forefathers resided there for twelve
years. But they were not at home. More than
all, they felt for their children, who were drawn
away from their pious practices by the temptations
of the great city and the new land. For their
sake, more than for their own, they desired another country, though it were a wilderness and the
home of savage men. They looked longingly
across the floods to the new world; they thought
that there they might be the founders of a realm

in which the greatest blessings would be secured for their posterity. Religious freedom was to them the greatest possession, and they were willing to encounter the sea, the wilderness, the savage, any perils, that they might have it.

At length, overcoming many obstacles, after many prayers, with the blessing of their pastor, who was left behind with the majority of the flock, they left the shores of Holland, and the white cliffs of England, one hundred and two souls on the *Mayflower*. They did not look back, but their eyes, during all their long voyage, were strained toward the west, the land of promise, to which across the flood they believed their God was leading them.

Dwelling in these cultured cities and towns of ours, where our Puritan civilization has been doing its work for almost two centuries and a half, it is not easy to grasp the greatness of their adventure who first settled on these shores. It was in the midst of a New England winter when they debarked. Houses were to be reared, fuel provided, food in some way obtained. Around them was the wilderness, its unknown recesses crowded with savages. They were to be workmen; they were also to be soldiers. Women and children were to be provided for. Everything crowded upon them and there were many obstacles, in the season, in their want of supplies, in their lack of boats and other necessary things. Sickness came, and almost one half of their number were sadly buried. At times nearly all of the little colony were prostrated so that not more than six or seven persons were able to wait upon the sick and bury the dead It seemed as though they were to be swept away. But there were stout hearts among them who bore up in the strength of the Lord.

At length the weary winter wore away. The birds sang in the forests, the brooks leaped in their shining channels, the sunshine started the emerald verdure; spring gushed over New England and the warm light shimmered on its seas. The lone survivors took heart.

Early in April, the *Mayflower* weighed anchor, shook out its furled sails to the breeze and with the half of its crew who had survived the winter, pointed its prow toward old England. Not a solitary emigrant returned in the vessel. Gloomy as the winter had been, severe as was the promise for the future, they stood firmly by their new settlement. It was not a rash adventure upon which they had come to these coasts. They were moved by manly and religious principle, and difficulties did not deter them. In their own lofty language they held " that all great and honorable actions are accompanied with great difficulties, and must be both enterprised and overcome with answerable courages." Before they were reinforced fifty-one,

just one half of their number, were laid with
the dead.

Such was the first chapter in New England history. England was great and prosperous. Peace
and plenty dwelt in all the kingdom. No happier
land lay beneath the sun. But there were Englishmen, who, though they prized these material
and social blessings, prized one thing higher.
Liberty! What were all other things without that?
Too well had they studied the Bible, too well had
they read the history of the past, too well had they
cherished the rights of Englishmen, to accept any
lower boon in the place of that. For sweet and
holy liberty they would abandon all that old,
happy, enlightened England could give them;
they would court the perils of the sea and the
wilderness and the heathen. The emigration to
New England went on. From Holland, from the
towns of England, great numbers came over to join
their brethren and friends.

They were a noble class of men who engaged in
the planting of New England. There are persons
who decry the forefathers, who reproach the Puritans. There are those even who inherit the blessings which they procured for them who vilify the
noble men to whom they owe the liberty which
they have to slander them! There are those who
enjoy the privileges which they owe to our fathers
who seem to take a horrid pleasure in saying

things derogatory of Puritanism. There are even
sons of the Puritans, inheritors of their names and
their institutions and their estates, who seem to
forget their fathers and what they owe to them.   I
wish to recall to you, my hearers, and to impress
especially upon my young friends, as we stand
again at this anniversary of the landing of the Pilgrims, the nobility and virtue and heroic deeds of
our honored forefathers. They loved England,
but they loved freedom and God more.   They
prized the churches and universities and homes of
their native land, but they prized a free conscience
and free worship more.   They might have enjoyed
as much in England as any of those whom they
left there, if they had been willing to conform to
the unjust demands of the state and the church.
All honor to them for their cheerful sacrifices
and patient fortitude !

Bradford, the first governor of the Plymouth
colony, was a man of literary taste, familiar with
the French and Dutch, the Greek and Latin
tongues, and taking special delight in the Hebrew
language.   Brewster, second to him, was in honor
at home, and, in the train of the English ambassador in Holland, had himself held the keys of
the Dutch towns that were in some respects bound
to England.   Winslow was a gentleman of fine
qualities, who, while traveling in Holland, became
acquainted with the eminent pastor, Robinson, and

attached himself to his church and its future fortunes. Robinson himself was a superior scholar and speaker, and in Leyden, was where the university founded by William the Silent, in memory of the heroic siege and honored with the names upon its rolls, of such scholars as Grotius, Scaliger, Arminius, and Descartes he received the attention of learned professors and preachers. Standish, the bold captain, was a military man of experience and promotion before he came to New England, and was the heir of large estates at home.

Skelton and Higginson were educated at Cambridge University and were non-conformist clergymen of the Church of England. White had been for many years rector of Trinity Church in Dorchester, and was widely esteemed. Endicott was a gentleman of parts and property, and there were associated with him, intending to follow him to America, nobles and men of wealth and education. The members of the Massachusetts company, pledged to embark for New England, were men of high position and character. Winthrop, whose immediate ancestors were lawyers, was a gentleman with an income equivalent to ten thousand dollars a year now, and moved in high circles at home. Humphrey, well-born, learned and godly, and Johnson, a man of large wealth, were both sons-in-law of the Earl of Lincoln. Sir Richard Saltonstall was one of them. Dudley was

an old soldier of character who had served in foreign parts.   Eaton had been a minister of the
crown to Denmark.   Bradstreet, the son of a clergyman, had studied at Cambridge.   Vassall was
a wealthy West India proprietor.   Hooker, Stone
and Cotton were divines who would have adorned
the ranks of the clergy in any land and age,
"men," says the historian of New England, "of
eminent capacity and sterling character, fit to be
concerned in the founding of a state."   And he
adds, "In all its generations of worth and refinement, Boston has never seen an assembly more
illustrious for generous qualities or manly culture,
than when the magistrates of the young colony
welcomed Cotton and his fellow voyagers at Winthrop's table."   This illustrious preacher brought
with him to our Boston the great fame which his
talents and learning had given him as the minister
of the ancient church of St. Botolph in Boston in
old England.   From that "superb temple," "a
cathedral in size and beauty," he "came to preach
the gospel within the mud walls and under the
thatched roof of the meeting-house in a rude New
England hamlet."

Such was the quality of our forefathers.   Their
clergy were mainly graduates of the universities of
Oxford and Cambridge.   Their magistrates were
men of character, rank and erudition.   Their common men were freemen with big English hearts

beating within their waistcoats. If anybody wants
a better ancestry he shall go far to find it. With
them came fair and noble ladies, and earnest-
hearted and devout dames, from the English homes
that they had adorned.   One of our chroniclers
says of Lady Arbella Johnson, that she came
"from a paradise of plenty and pleasure, which
she enjoyed in the family of a noble earldom, into
a wilderness of wants." They were women who
were worthy to be the mothers of nations.   With
no regrets did they look back to the comforts and
enjoyments they had left, but with true hearts they
cheered their husbands and sons in the manly
work which they had in hand.

We may judge of the character of our forefathers by their associates who remained in England
to battle there for the same principles which led
them over the seas.   They belonged to the same
class with those who not long after overturned the
ancient monarchy and founded the majestic commonwealth.   In sympathy with them was a large
part of the ancient nobility of the kingdom.   The
landed gentry and the moneyed class were largely
with them.   When the contest in arms came on,
such nobles as Manchester, Essex, Warwick,
Brooke and Fairfax commanded the Puritan
armies and fleets.   Lord Say and Seal and Lord
Brooke, after whom was named our Saybrook,
both designed to come to New England.   John

Hampden, that illustrious commoner, the grandest
Englishman of the age, also, at one time, thought
of emigrating to these shores.   The members of
the Massachusetts company who remained in England became, some of them members of parlia-
ment.   Others who were interested in New England became officers in the army of the people
against the crown, judges, who pronounced deci-
sions on the trial of the king, statesmen, who
molded the affairs of the Revolution.   The first
scholars of England were of the Puritans.   Selden,
Lightfoot, Gale and Owen were among them.
The finest preachers were in their ranks.   Colonel
Hutchinson was an accomplished and godly representative of them.   Many of the most learned
lawyers were with them.   Milton, splendid in personal appearance and in mental accomplishments,
a poet equal to Homer, a scholar learned in ancient
and modern lore, devoted his fine faculties to the
Puritan cause.   These men, and such as these, were
among the most accomplished, as they were among
the most opulent and noble of Englishmen.   Royal-
ists and churchmen have attempted to disparage
them and have heaped ridicule upon their memory.
But royalist and churchman found more than their
match whether they met them in the contest of
arms or of debate.   There was little ridicule at
Marston Moor, Dunbar and Worcester, when
the Puritan legions bore down the king's forces in

terrible battle. It needed more than a king to withstand Cromwell, and there was not a royalist who was the peer of his Latin secretary.

If there had not been so much to do at home, had not England required the presence of so many of her best men, had not the assertion and defence of freedom on English soil itself checked the emigration, thousands more of eminent and accomplished men would have thronged to New England to lay here the foundations of a commonwealth grander than then existed.

This was what our forefathers wanted. They wanted to set up on these shores a nation of freemen, to plant here a New England which, in all the best qualities of a state, should surpass the old. They, and those who sympathized with them at home held the sublime purpose to erect an empire which should fulfill their holiest and most patriotic longings, where their thought and worship should be free and God should be their only Lord. With tender affection they said on leaving England: " We esteem it our honor to call the Church of England, from whence we rise, our dear mother, and cannot part from our native country, where she specially resideth, without much sadness of heart and many tears in our eyes."

So they came. I cannot to-day describe their growth, their stern battling with difficulty and disaster, their unconquerable purpose, and their triumphant progress; how the wilderness fell before them, and the savage fled, how agriculture covered the hills with its products, and commerce whitened the shores with its sails; how villages grew to cities, and wealth accumulated; how schools were planted, and steepled churches rose in every hamlet, and universities were opened for liberal culture; how the town and the state took the forms of freedom; how a Christian aristocracy was cherished, and how all were combined in a free and beautiful commonwealth.

But if you would know what they accomplished, I can tell you in the language which one used to him, who, standing beneath the dome of St. Peter's, asked for the monument of its builder, "Look around you!" New England is the memorial and monument of the forefathers. Were an impartial and intelligent cosmopolitan to point to that people among whom thrift and virtue and intelligence and education and religion were most largely diffused, would not his finger designate New England on the world's map?

I am speaking to-day to descendants of these forefathers. In honoring them I am placing the crown upon your heads. For "the glory of children are their fathers."

You are reminded in viewing them of your duty. Cherish then and maintain the churches that they planted here. Flung upon the new world, they cast away the human ecclesiastical inventions. Papacy and episcopacy they left behind them. God's Word they brought with them. And taking that alone as a guide, with their own good sense, they founded Congregational churches like those of which they read in the New Testament. Christ's churches were sufficient for them; churches for the intelligent duties of men and women in the worship of God. They would have no miter nor canon, no priest nor pope. They would call no man master. They would have no authority higher than the Bible. As freemen in the Lord, each one equal to another before Him who looks down on all men as worms of the dust, they entered into mutual covenant in the Church of Christ, promising to watch over and care for each other. I commend to you, then, by the example and sufferings of your fathers, these our Congregational churches. They are yours through what your fathers have endured. Stand by them with something of their fidelity and sacrifice. Give to them a generous enthusiasm and affection. Let not the church languish, whatever else may languish. No organization, no business is so important and worthy as the church. Congregational churches and Republican liberties stand and flourish together.

Cherish also their love of freedom and be ready to make efforts like theirs to maintain it. We have fallen upon times that need the example of

the forefathers. Liberty is in peril. Manhood is
at a discount. There is danger lest we shall go
down upon our knees before the Dragon of slavery.
There is danger lest in seeking to hold the smaller
good we shall lose the greater.

Our fathers loved the union between Old and
New England. But they would not become slaves
to maintain it. Truth and liberty were better than
it. The mutterings and threats of the tyrants had
no terrors for them. They only stirred up the
more their manhood and independence. We, in
these times, should imitate them. Through the
gloom and conflicts of their life in England, on the
track of the storm-tossed *Mayflower*, amidst the
hardships of the first New England winter, in the
work of laying well the foundations of a new commonwealth, we may find stimulants to a devotion to good principles, whatever may be the
temptations to swerve from them, whoever may
forfeit his birthright.

And let us ever thank God that New England is
ours. Its rigorous climate, its hardy soil, its sea-
dashed coasts, its tempests, its mountains, its pro-
ductions are the nutriments of manhood. They
tend to develop a bold and brawny race; they
cherish the grandest qualities of human nature.
Work, hard work is our lot, and it is in itself a
first-rate inheritance. Our mountain battlements
are the fortresses of freedom.

Shame to us, if, spurred by the daring and deeds of our forefathers, we degenerate into cravens and slaves! Rather let us be as the Puritans. "They knew they were pilgrims and looked not much on those things, but lift up their eyes to the heavens, their dearest country, and quieted their spirits."

In a more southern latitude and within the civilization of the followers of William Penn, I give this tribute to our forefathers. There is much that is admirable in the soberness and simplicity and unconformity to the world of the Society of the Friends. And that is a fine civilization which is planted on the shores of the Delaware and which is illustrated in the social life and the learning and the business and the eleemosynary institutions of the city of Philadelphia, which in many respects is the first city of the land. But for that which is noblest in manhood and most graceful in womanhood, for the wisdom and energy which go forth in most successful achievement, for the principles which underlie the best construction of society, I turn to our own New England Puritanism, it may be with a filial spirit, but yet with the consciouness that the honest cosmopolitan would agree with me. I have ever held, even at personal sacrifice and loss, that we who go out from the home-land should carry our precious principles with us and whether we migrate to the South or follow the

broad courses of commerce and population to the
West, which is rising with imperial grandeur to the
control of the continent, we should be of New
England still, our hearts beating ever in harmony
with those who remain behind and that we all
should hold, with sacred regard, to the institutions
which were bequeathed to us by our noble forefathers.

RUTH AS AN EXAMPLE TO YOUNG DISCIPLES

And Ruth said, Intreat me not to leave thee, and to return from following after thee : for whither thou goest, I will go ; and where thou lodgest, I will lodge : thy people shall be my people, and thy God my God : where thou diest, will I die, and there will I be buried : the Lord do so to me, and more also, if aught but death part thee and me.—*The Book of Ruth* 1 : 16, 17.

———

GRAND AVENUE, NEW HAVEN.

RUTH AS AN EXAMPLE TO YOUNG DISCIPLES

It is told of Dr. Franklin, that, being in the company of some noble and worldly ladies, with whom, as the representative of this country in its heroic beginnings, he was quite a favorite, he proposed to read to them a pleasant idyl. They gladly acquiesced, expecting the grave but charming philosopher to beguile them by what he might offer. He took the Bible, which was a strange and unread volume to them, and read the Book of Ruth. They were delighted with the idyllic story and wondered where the doctor had discovered such a gem. It would be difficult to find in all literature anything of the kind more beautiful than this artless history, or more fruitful of lessons of most suggestive wisdom.

The sweet name of Ruth has stood next to that of the mother of our Lord in the affectionate regard of his people for many centuries; indeed, she was herself the mother of our Lord, as being the ancestress, in that far-off age, of David and of Christ. She gives us a rare example of conversion to the

true God, in an age and among a people given over
to idolatry; she was one of the earliest, as she was
one of the truest, of the great multitudes brought
into the Church from the Gentile nations, and so
was the prophetess of the world's harvest for
Christ; she was a figure of heroic beauty in the
annals of God's people; she was a singular illustration of the methods of divine Providence in the
world and of the care of God for his own; while
her simple biography sets forth the homely life and
the manners of the days and the people with which
her story is interwoven.

And there are still broader lessons in this prose
poem. We are taught that humble individuals
are often God's chosen agents for the accomplishment of divine purposes; that the lowliest families
rank with the most princely on the heraldry of
heaven; that this life to all of us may be a life of
marvel or calamity; that through whatever we
may pass, an unfaltering trust in the overruling
Providence will bring its ample reward; that we
need never to despair, however dark our experiences may be, into whatever personal or domestic
afflictions we may be plunged; that blessed recompenses are bestowed on self-denial and cross-bearing, and the noble performance of duty; that we
can go nowhere with God and with the people of
God without being on the joyful journey toward
the place of which the Lord has said, " I will give

it you;" and that so good will come to us, "for
the Lord hath spoken good concerning Israel."
But without dwelling on these wide and volumi-
nous and instructive lessons of the sacred narrative, I wish to-day to direct your thought to Ruth,
as an example to the young disciple.

First, we notice that there was a great *renunciation* on her part, of much that she must have
valued, for the sake of being with God's people.
She had been brought up in Moab.   Her fair girlhood had all been spent among the idolaters.
There was her home.   There were her parents,
and her brothers and sisters and many friends.
She was used to the worship of the god Chemosh.
The rich and productive plains of Moab, the popu-
lous and powerful cities of that courageous nation,
which had descended from Lot, were familiar to
her.   Her education and all her associations were
among that people.

For her then to turn away from all these, that
she might ally herself to the friends and people of
God, involved a renunciation of everything which
had been dear to her.   She must leave home, dearest kindred, early associates, the altars of her childhood, priests who had instructed her in the rites
of their dark religion, the playgrounds and the
playmates of her beautiful girlhood, the landscapes,
like pictures, on which her sight had reveled, and
the skies that had always bent over her with their

starry glories.   It was to say a long farewell to
her treasures of love and memory and hope.   But
she renounced them all.   With tears in her dark
eyes and a shadow on her face of beauty, and a
gloom in her heroic soul, she turned her back forever upon her happy past, upon her old pleasures
and her old associates, upon her early religion and
her early home.   With a pathos unsurpassed in
human speech she said, as she turned away from
the old and clung to the new: "Whither thou
goest, I will go; and where thou lodgest, I will
lodge: thy people shall be my people, and thy
God my God."

So did she become an example to the young
disciple of every age and place.   It costs something to be a Christian.   Our Lord has put it
among the foremost of his instructions to those
who would follow him that they are to have an
experience of renunciation.   Old things are to
pass away.   All things are to become new.   Love
for him must be so strong that other things, even
dearest friends, must be hated in the comparison.
We must love not the world, nor the things that
are in the world.   Our love to God must be so supreme that the love of the world and the love of
friends cannot stand against it.   We must be not
conformed to this world, but must be transformed,
so that our affections shall be set not on things on
the earth but on heavenly things.   The apostle

said of himself and of those who were with him in the Christian service, "We have renounced the hidden things of shame;" we have openly declared ourselves off from the old life; we have disowned it. This great principle of renunciation is fundamental and all-important in the creed and in the practice of the young disciple. If he cannot declare himself off from his sinful practices and disown his sinful associates, and leave everything behind him that stands in the way of his joining the people of God, he will not be a full and round Christian; he may fail, in the end, of being a Christian at all.

This, I say, is fundamental and all-important. It is especially so in our day, when a soft and easy religion is in vogue, when the line of distinction between the world and the Church is so shadowy, when young Christians are liable to take up with pretence for reality. Let them ask themselves, Am I willing to renounce and disown anything, everything, that comes in the way of my confession of Christ? Let them hold before themselves the example of the Moabite maiden, who, in that far-away age and among that nation of pagans, turned her back upon all old things, that she might live and die with the people of God. We want Ruths in our day,—young disciples of brave and self-denying devotion. We have them, but we want more of them. We want the Church filled

with earnest maidens and their brothers, who cannot be kept back from heroic consecration, who
will go with God's people, who will say, " Thy
people shall be my people, and thy God my God :
where thou diest, will I die, and there will I be
buried ; " who thus will be Christ's, living and
dying, everywhere and wholly Christ's.

Secondly, we notice that there was a cordial
reception on her part of the obligations which
belonged to the choice of the true religion. There
was renunciation of some things, there was reception of other things. She did not waver. She was
in no uncertain and doubtful mood. There was no
question in her mind where she belonged. Orpah,
who set out with her " on the way to return unto
the land of Judah," kissed her mother-in-law, and
went back unto her people and unto her god.
The old attraction was too strong. She merely
set out, and soon went back. And so it is with
many who appear to start for the heavenly land.
They are serious ; they pray ; they consort with
the people of God for a few weeks or months, and
then they return to their old habits and their old
associates. They think they have tried religion,
but they know nothing of it. There are many
Orpahs.

Naomi proposed to Ruth that she, too, should
return, should follow her sister-in-law. But Ruth
had chosen the good part, not hesitatingly, not

doubtfully, not in a half-hearted way; but fully
and cordially and with decision. "And Ruth said,
Intreat me not to leave thee, and to return from
following after thee: for whither thou goest, I
will go; and where thou lodgest, I will lodge: thy
people shall be my people, and thy God my God:
where thou diest, will I die, and there will I be
buried." This was a full reception of the Hebrew
faith and of the true God, and a cordial and glad
union to the people of God. It was not merely a
love for her gentle mother, Naomi. She loved
Naomi, for there was much that was lovable in
her. Ten years of life with her, in their home in
Moab, had shown Ruth the sweetness of her disposition not only, but the excellence of her religion as well. Her daily reading of the Scriptures
of her people, her daily prayers to the unseen but
present God of her fathers, the sublime hope she
cherished of the Consolation of Israel, the holy
submission with which she had endured the loss of
her husband and her sons, the calm faith with
which she looked forward to a blessed reunion
with them and with all the people of God in the
glorious place of which the Lord said, "I will
give it you," had won the heart of Ruth not only
to herself but to her God, also.

The piety of Naomi was the instrumentality
which God used to save the fair maiden of Moab
and to give her courage and determination and

grace in open and whole-souled confession of her
faith and union to God's people. The reason why
so many young disciples halt and hesitate and
seem afraid to commit themselves, and stand shivering on the brink of a confession, is that the old
Christians are such weak and inefficient professors.
The inconsistency and irregularity and worldliness
of old professors intimidate and discourage young
believers. Is that all there is of religion? they
say. Is that the way to follow Christ? Isn't
there any more to it than such weakness and irres-
olution? Does Christianity permit its professors
to neglect the church and the sacraments and the
prayer-meeting, and to go to the theater and the
sociable and the moral reform meeting, to abandon the one Cause for the sake of some secondary
object; to devote the best time and the freshest
energies to the outside matter, and to give the
dregs and remnants to Christ, or to give him the
go-by altogether? And so the young disciple is
perplexed and hindered and never matures. If
you want Ruths, you must have Naomis. If you
want young Christians who will stand forth in the
Christian order and in the courage of earnest convictions, you must have old Christians whose lives
will square with the precepts and principles of
Christ. You can't expect sturdy offspring from
decayed parentage. You can't look for heroic
faith in the disciples of a lax and unbelieving

church.   Your converts will be about such as you
are.

Yet Ruth should be their example.   If possible,
the converts should look away from living illustrations, if they are poor illustrations, of religion, to
those who are worthy of imitation, even if they
lived long ago.   The brightness of their example
illumines our path of duty.   The world will never
grow so old that the sweetness and courage and
constancy of the dauntless Ruth shall be unworthy
of imitation.   She received God and her whole
duty to him into her soul of souls.   Her receptive
mind took in the people of God and life with them
and death with them ; it took in sacrifice and self-
denial and cross-bearing and separation from
friends and the world.   God and God's people
and their holy life and death were all in all to her.

Thirdly, we notice that she welcomed the rich
recompenses which rewarded and crowned her
fidelity.   On the first page of the New Testament,
in the ancestral line of the world's foremost Man,
the world's divine-human Redeemer, is the name of
Ruth.   Honors were hers such as few have
achieved or received.   She came, with the gentle
Naomi, to Bethlehem, and lent something of renown to that most renowned of the world's famous
places.   From her quiet home her name and her
fame went out through all the land of Judah, and
all that she had done in leaving her father and her

14

mother and the land of her nativity, and coming
to a strange people and accepting the true God,
under whose wings she had come to take refuge,
was told among Hebrew maidens and men, in her
praise.   She became the wife of one of the foremost Hebrews. She stood high among the matrons
of Israel and had all that wealth and station could
give her.   She was the mother of a son who became the ancestor of Christ.   That greatest honor
of Hebrew motherhood, for which the mothers of
Israel longed and prayed, that theirs might be the
parentage of Him in whom their own people and
all the nations of the earth were to be blessed, was
the crowning glory of Ruth.   Her faith, which God
gave her for his service, her noble resolve, by
which she cast away all her paganism and threw
herself with all the wealth of her affection and the
devotion of her life into the love of God and into
union with his people, the sacrifice by which she
rent herself from her dearest friends and bound
herself to strangers who were of God's family, had
the grandest recompense.   The sweet name of
Ruth is in honor in all the world, it is in glory in
the heavenly world.   She took God for her God
with all her heart.   She took God's people for her
people with a daughter's loving trust.   With them
she would live, with them she would die.   She
honored God, and God, according to his word,
honored her.

There is a recompense of reward, and all may have it who choose God fully and serve him faithfully. But we cannot halt nor waver nor refuse to fulfil any one of the commandments which he lays upon us.

Ruth left all, but she gained all. To her was fulfilled the remarkable sayings of her Son and her Lord: "There is no man that hath left house, or brethren, or sisters, or mother, or father, or children, or lands, for my sake, and for the gospel's sake, but he shall receive a hundredfold now in this time, . . . with persecutions; and in the world to come eternal life."

"Where thou diest, will I die, and there will I be buried." Only death should separate them. We love God's people in life; we would be buried with them when we die; we would also rise with them in the great resurrection day.

You have read of the slaughter of the brave Italian troops in the gorge of Dogali, in which five hundred and eighty men were surprised by ten thousand Abyssinian troops who poured a withering fire upon them until every Italian soldier was killed or wounded, but not till, with heroic courage, they had destroyed five thousand of the treacherous enemy. The wounded wished to come home and to die and be buried in the soil of their loved Italy and under her brilliant skies and by the graves of kindred.

You have read how a few weeks ago Italy welcomed them. It was in the beautiful harbor of Naples that the warship rode at anchor that had brought them home. The city was thronged with people. More than half a million of citizens from all parts of the kingdom crowded the streets and the houses to their tops. The schools were dismissed, and all business was suspended. Banners, draped and mournful, hung on every hand. Leaves of oak and laurel covered the pavements, emblems of victorious courage. Only petals of roses and lilies and beautiful flowers of a sunny clime were permitted to be showered upon the heroes. At noon, when the cannon of the castle thundered forth the hour, a silence, like the silence of a petrified city, fell upon all the bands of music and all the great processions and all the inhabitants, while from the wharf to the hospital the ambulance-wagons passed through the smiling and weeping and sympathetic multitudes who so welcomed home their wounded brothers. Citizens of noblest rank, officers of highest grade, with humble toilers and with mothers and little children, wept and rejoiced and loved.

"Thy people shall be my people, and thy God my God: where thou diest will I die, and there will I be buried."

XII

THE ORNAMENT OF WOMAN

"Favour is deceitful. and beauty is vain : but a woman that feareth the Lord. she shall be praised."—*The Proverbs* 31 : 30.

———

GRAND AVENUE, NEW HAVEN.

THE ORNAMENT OF WOMAN

I had occasion a few Sabbaths ago to speak of some of the adverse tendencies working in our times on the minds of young women, and I specified a lack of thought, a lack of truthfulness, waste of time, undue desire for personal adornment, the passion for social excitements, the unrelieved slavery in necessary duty.

Notwithstanding these tendencies which are adverse, and which are in many cases potent and effective, so that many young women are lured into lives which are a discredit to them, there are yet many who respond to other propitious and elevating influences and look forth upon this life as holding in it achievements and noblest conquests for themselves.

The position of a young woman is one of special peculiarity. It is quite unlike that of a young man. To him the world is open. He is free to go. He is free to choose. The paths of life are manifold on which he may walk, and the positions manifold to which he may aspire. Her position is one of greater dependence and greater solitariness.

If she abides in the home of her childhood, the
child-feeling remains strong with her; if she ven-
tures out into employment for herself she is re-
stricted to narrow bounds of service and of pleasure. However boldly she may propose to act,
there will come the constant suggestion that she
cannot be too independent in her feelings or her
endeavors. She needs sympathy and fellowship
and love. Yet her task is her own, and on most
of the way that she chooses for herself she has to
be alone; she cannot admit too much confidence
nor betray her individual preferences to unsympa-
thetic natures. But these facts of comparative
dependence and solitariness awaken concern and
sympathy. We cannot look upon the young
women of our society without care and hope for
their future.

I am to speak to-day of that which is the real
ornament of the young woman.

" Favour is deceitful, and beauty is vain: but a
woman that feareth the Lord, she shall be praised."
It does not consist then in outward loveliness or
beauty. These things have their charm. These
have been used for ages as the wand of woman's
power. There is a spell in them over the mind
and heart of the grosser sex. The most urgent
prayer of the Greek mother was for the beauty of
her children. One of the great lawyers of Athens,
defending the most beautiful woman of that city,

who was accused of corrupting its youth, secured
her acquittal by suddenly unveiling her before the
dazzled judges.   The chisels of the great sculptors
wrought the Parian marble into forms of highest
physical perfection.   The admiration of beauty
became a passion of the people.

Yet vice and beauty were closely connected;
the loveliest faces were enamelled masks over corrupt hearts; public courtesans were models of the
matchless statues; the sacred temples received
their choicest adornment from the forms of the
most degenerate women.   So was it seen that favor
is deceitful and beauty is vain.   Great as is their
charm, these are not the real ornament of woman.
These may consist with depraved tastes, with dis-
graceful habits, with indecent impurities.

Beauty is not to be despised; it is the wonderful gift of God.   But if it makes its possessor vain,
if it is merely of the surface, if it has no corres-
pondence in the soul, it is a useless charm, alluring but deceiving.   Real beauty is of the mind.
To lead this forth, to give the mind reach and
grasp, to discipline its faculties, to elevate its
desires, to make it strong to do and to endure, to
enlarge its knowledge that it may use wisely its
experience is the first necessity of the young
woman of our day.   *Education is real ornament.*
Mind is more than body.   When care is given ex-
clusively to the latter, when this is adorned with

all that taste can suggest and wealth can furnish, while the former is neglected, there is a dreadful waste of effort and expenditure.

The first thing is the mind. The gem is more than the casket that holds it. The casket may be rough and ungainly, the diamond will glow and throb with light just as splendidly within it. It would be a waste to beautify and enrich the case which was to hold only a common pebble. In acquiring the best possible education our young women are simply doing justice to themselves. They are fortunate in living in this day, when the worth and privilege and desirableness of the best culture are freely accorded to them, when the colleges are opening their doors to them, or when their own colleges are giving them equal advantages with those of their brothers.

There is no dispute, or there ought to be no dispute, as to the equality of men and women in their mental constitution. God has made each sex for itself and for the other. It is not good that either should be alone. One is the complement of the other. They have the same mental faculties, intellect, susceptibilities, will, conscience, power. The same studies invite them. Histories have been made alike for them. The unexplored territories of science, whether in the globe beneath us or in the astronomical worlds that silently roll above us, are the inviting domain of

both. Each can work on the mighty problems
that are stated in consciousness or evolved in
human experience. The throne of England is
strong under its sensible queen. The telescope
does not hold back its revelations when pointed
by Miss Mitchell. Music, in its wealth of melody
and harmony, reveals its fascination through the
voices of many female singers. Letters bear the
unchallenged stamp of the genius of woman, in
poetry, in romance, in philosophy, in science. In
the galleries of the Louvre, in the medical halls
of Vienna, among the glaciers of the Alps, women are taking hold of tasks which prove their
ability to cope with men in discovery and achievement.

The young woman of this time should not be
satisfied till she has accomplished a liberal education. If beyond that she can attain proficiency in
some calling, in art, in music, in teaching, in writing, in housewifery, in some trades that are open
to her, in positions that she may seize with original audacity and hold with original ability,
the greater will be her acquisition of real ornament. It is a disgrace to the higher civilization that women are not accorded equality in
rights and in rewards with men for that which they
are equally competent to do and equally efficient
in doing. Sex should not be the gauge of wages;
good work and success, by whomsoever achieved,

should be the gauge. This result is to be gained
by the persistent effort of one sex and the growing
sense of justice of the other sex. Independence
will come from proficiency in some substantial
calling, and in that is real adornment.

There is a sphere of noble duty for which
woman is eminently commissioned, the sphere of
charity for the unfortunate. The Romish communion sets apart for this work a separated order,
under lasting vows, of devoted Sisters of Charity,
whose life is spent in works of sympathy and alleviation. Our Protestant churches have the sisterhood
without, badge or vow, voluntarily taking upon
themselves the same tasks and manifesting the same
intrepidity and self-denial. But the service should
be more general. Every young woman who would
have the fairest adorning should be a member of
this open order to which is given the honor of dis-
pensing mercy, in seeking out the sorrowful and
needy, in supplying bread to the hungry in body
and in soul, in doing real sisterly work for the little
children who are poor and distressed for the want
of love. Pity, pity like that of Christ should be
the beautiful ornament of our daughters, crowd-
ing aside by its inspiring motives the listless, aimless insipidity with which so many young women
fill up their lives. Let theirs be the work of
benevolence which shall visit every house with ben-
efaction of some sort. Let theirs be the privilege

of sustaining the cause of temperance, rejecting and frowning upon bad and demoralizing drinking habits, holding aloof with unswerving severity every one who is not willing to abandon intoxicating beverages, and proving that that society is of a finer sort and purer character which has its basis in total abstinence.

Personal religion is the brightest ornament of a young woman. It is all wrong to see a young man coming on in life destitute of religious principle, but the sight of a young woman without religion is still more repugnant. Christianity has done everything to elevate and bless the womanhood. Women were slaves without it. They were beasts of burden without it. But under its sanctifying principles they have taken their place by the side of men, they have received kindness and deference and love, they have been treated with more than chivalric devotion. Gratitude should lead them to Christ, and Christ has had their love and faith. The records of all churches are bright with the supreme consecration of women. The dark annals of martyrdom attest their constancy to Christ. Christ has done everything for them, they have withheld nothing from him. Agitated by the problems of life, the young woman needs religion for her personal peace. She needs it for the friendship to which it introduces her. She needs it for the blessed work which it assigns to her.

The youth, unused to the world's ways, uncertain of the future, looking toward eternity, seeks direction and protection, and this is found in Christ. The young woman who walks with him, whose inexperience and earnestness are controlled by him, cannot be lonely nor disheartened ; she has a present Friend who is strong and trustworthy, whose love brightens all her days.

And her work is ever at hand. The anxiety and misery of an aimless life are taken away from her. In the home which she blesses with her sunny presence, in the offices of instruction and example with which she seeks to lead the younger sisters of her household or of other households, the groups which gather near to her in the Sunday-school, in the charity with which she ministers to the miserable who welcome her as an angel from the skies, in the daily benediction which she pours upon her path for the comfort and strength and cheer of others, as the sun never fails to rise, she illustrates the beauty of a life ordered in harmony with the will of her Lord. She lives with a great and inspiring aim. She has nothing to wait for, as others seem to have, for her life is full, Christ is in it, and he ennobles and sanctifies it. She has peace and her sleep is that of the blessed. She has possessions, unfading, immortal, and friendship, and stainless ambition, and her work is by the side of the blessed Master.

Such I take to be the real ornament of the young woman: education, proficiency in some calling, charity, religion. These are more than any outward adorning of plaiting the hair, or wearing of gold, or putting on of apparel. These are the enduring befitments of female character. Much is said in our day of the rights of women, and some young women have thrown themselves, with fine gifts, into the discussion and evolution of that subject. But there are unquestioned rights which will be always accorded without publicity or revolution or warfare and which are infinitely superior to any that belong to the platform or the polls.

Florence Nightingale was applauded in securing the rights she needed to become the alleviator of the suffering and the dying on many battle-fields, and to appropriate a quarter of a million of dollars to found a hospital for nurses who should be stimulated to philanthropic work by her name and example.

The baroness Burdett-Coutts has needed no endorsement as to her rights in devoting her time and her fortune to the improvement of the homes and the habits of the poor. The young ladies who have gone from Mt. Holyoke Seminary to Southern Africa to plant on the rescued soil of heathenism an African Holyoke, in which the daughters of that region may be trained for worthy lives, have felt no solicitude as to being accorded their rights.

Nor have their sisters, from the days of Harriet Newell to the time when the last zenana welcomed the daughter of one of our families to be light and help in its darkness and misery. The great number of our own young women, who, under the stress of hard necessity or from the heroic sentiment of independence, have taken upon them the tasks of instruction and have carried into the schools a sublime consecration which works beyond the outwards tasks in seeking to make noble the lives of their pupils here and to fit them for the immortalities hereafter, have no trouble in determining their personal rights, find in hand all that they have ability to achieve.

The motive which has its impelling power in love to Christ, and from that, in love for the souls that are to be saved, heightens beyond all else the beauty and charm of the life of woman. There is much of excellence in the womanhood of the highest types set before us in the history and poetry of ancient Greece; as in the wifely constancy of Penelope waiting for twenty long years for her absent husband to return from the Trojan war; the tenderness of Andromache for her heroic husband; the sisterly devotion of Antigone, and in the virtues of many others whose lives may, however, partake more of fable than of fact. But the redemption of Christ has been eminently the redemption of woman; it has changed the nature

of her relations and the sphere of her services; it
has sanctified her generous impulses and broad-
ened her self-denying activities.

Six Roman virgins were selected to keep a perpetual fire on the altar of the temple of Vesta. The
safety of the city, the welfare of every home,
depended on the continuance of that fire. Night
and day they were the faithful watchers of the
ceaseless flame. If it went out their punishment
was severe, and it could be kindled again only from
the sun. It is a type of the influence lodged in
the young women of the land. I believe the safety
of society, the well-being of our homes, the glory
of our institutions, are all dependent upon their
character and life. In their soft hands they hold
the silver sickles with which our harvests of good
or of evil are to be gathered. Vice cannot last in
the presence of their virtue. In the old legends
the fierce lion became docile, and the untamed
rhinoceros was fascinated before a virgin. If this
power fails us, if our young women do not fulfill
their responsibility, they will meet the fate of the
vestals; and we shall have to look to heaven in
prayer that the quenched fire may be kindled
again !

15

XIII

THE WORK OF WOMAN

" The Lord giveth the word: The women that publish the tidings are a great host."—*Psalms* 68 : 11.

———

GRAND AVENUE CHURCH, NEW HAVEN.

THE WORK OF WOMAN

More and more woman is coming to the front
in the progress of the Lord's kingdom on earth.
From the first, from time to time, there have been
individual instances of feminine heroism which
have left a great renown in history, and have sig-
nalized a few names as symbols, and prophetic of
what womanhood may achieve. The poet who
composed this verse was also a prophet. As a poet
he felt the inspiration of his people's past history.
One event stood grandly out in the imposing succession of wonders which had characterized the
career of Israel. It was the deliverance of the
nation from the power of Egypt. In the historic
pictures of that deliverance a female form emerged
on the canvas. It is that of Miriam. First, she
is standing on the banks of the Nile, keeping
watch over a little ark of bulrushes which was
floating among the flags, and in which lay a little
boy. By the command of the king that boy was
to die, but by the assurance of faith he was to live.
Only this Hebrew girl kept ward and watch over
him. No band of armed sentinels, not all the

power of Israel, could have been of any avail.
For Egypt was mighty. It was a lone maiden
watching through the long night with a devotion
that would not let her sleep, and with a patience
that was rewarded by the life of one who was to
become a great ruler in Egypt and the foremost
leader of God's people.

Again, she is standing on the shores of the Red
Sea. She has grown to womanhood. She has
become a prophetess. And that little boy whom
she saved is now leading the hundreds of thousands of his people forth from the Egyptian bondage. He is celebrating the overthrow of the
Egyptian hosts in the Red Sea, across which the
Hebrews have come on a dry path. And there
Miriam, in the inspiration of her vocation, with
flashing eye and dancing step, and voice that
mingled with the bass of the exulting sea, is leading the multitude of Hebrew women in their triumph and response, " Sing ye to the Lord, for he
hath triumphed gloriously; the horse and his
rider hath he thrown into the sea." The poet .re-
called these facts of history. He recalled also the
leadership of Deborah, who was a prophetess and
a judge of Israel, the saviour of her country from
the invasion of Sisera, "A mother in Israel," as
she styles herself, whose victorious pæan ends, " So
let all thine enemies perish, O Lord: but let them
that love him be as the sun when he goeth forth

in his might." He recalled, also, the heroic and self-sacrificing spirit of Esther (Stella), when for her people she most willingly took the risk of life or death, saying, " If I perish, I perish," and by her influence with the proud Persian monarch redeemed her whole nation from the slaughter which Haman had plotted against them. He recalled, too, that scene after David's victory over the Philistine, when the women came out of all the cities of Israel, singing and dancing, with timbrels, with joy, and with instruments of music, singing in their play, " Saul hath slain his thousands, and David his ten thousands." And, as the review of the past reminded him of the important part which the women had borne in the progress and victories of the chosen people, so his prophetic foresight assured him of that great work which they also were to do in the spread and triumph of the good cause in the future. The hosts of women who had celebrated with timbrels and joy and victorious psalms the conquests of the past, would be repeated in the gospel times by the mighty hosts of women who would take up the work of the Redeemer, and with a faith that should rival that of Miriam and Deborah and Rahab and Esther, would carry the gospel to the souls that are lost. And so, later on in the Psalm, foreseeing the full and final victory of Christ, he says, " The singers went before, the minstrels followed after, in the midst of the

damsels playing with timbrels. . . . Kings shall
bring presents unto thee. . . . Ethiopia shall
haste to stretch out her hands unto God. Sing
unto God, ye kingdoms of the earth." He fore-
sees in prophetic vision the triumph of the Word
in all the world. And this is to be brought about
largely through the efficiency of woman. "The
Lord giveth the word: The women that publish
the tidings are a great host."

We need not infer from this that there is to be
or that there needs to be, any great change in the
sphere of woman. Undoubtedly, the importance
that is given to woman's work and the significance
that is given to woman's mission may have turned
the heads, or dazzled the fancy, or spurred the
ambition, of some women, so that they have raised
a clamor for their rights, or set about the securing
of privileges, or sought positions of public leadership. But all this is confined to a narrow number.
And a little experience will be sufficient to con-
vince most women of good sense that their true
sphere, as the Bible defines it, and as their own
modesty would limit it, is all-sufficient for the best
use of all the powers and opportunities that they
possess. The right to vote, the right to mingle
in fierce political debate, the right to hold public
office and to bear public burdens, the right to be
morally unsexed,—such rights as these are not the
aim of the truest women. Their sphere, as it is,

is ample. It is noble, also. It is wide enough
and important enough to tax all the powers which
women possess, and it is a work of supererogation
on their part to seek for anything different or
greater. If there are women, in our day, or in
any day, who have some peculiar qualities of
public leadership, who are of eloquent speech, so
that they can move assemblies with exceptional
power, who are remarkable organizers, so that
they can plan victory, as it were, on a chart, as
Napoleon did, who have any extraordinary gift
which is useful and needed in the great good work,
let such women have room, let the world get the
benefit of their genius, if it be genius, let them
accomplish that which perhaps would not be accomplished but for their idiosyncracy. He would
be less than a man who would deny to them their
exceptional mission. But for women, as they are,
without noting the exceptions, the sphere, as it is,
is all right, and all that is wanted is the fulfilment
of women's work in it. The best women that I
know are not clamorers for novel rights, or new duties, or different spheres; they are only intent on
doing well what is now at their hand to do, and
are only anxious lest they cannot discharge that
which from all sides is pressing upon their sympathies and their womanly obligations. They have
no time, as they have no desire, to enter into the
hustings with men, or to squabble for political

place, or to lay aside the pure crown of their delicacy. They want no greater privilege, as there is no greater glory on earth than to be the Lord's faithful handmaidens in widening the blessings and victories of his kingdom. They are co-workers with the Lord not only, but with men as well. "The Lord giveth the word: The women that publish the tidings are a great host."

Relatively, their number is great. Two thirds of the Christians of the world are women. It sometimes seems as though Christianity had come to make good to women that of which they have been robbed by heathenism and false religions. By these they have been oppressed and tortured and reduced to slavery. They have been treated as the tool of man, as his beast of burden, and worse. Christianity has raised woman to her true place, as the equal and companion of man. She has found in Christ her best Friend, her omnipotent Deliverer. Christianity has awakened and intensified the spirit of chivalry in her behalf, so that woman has been the pride of man, the ornament of society, the queen in human affairs. And woman has repaid this regard and work of Christianity for her by the devotion and love and service and enthusiasm of her own life for Christ. She has returned love for love. The records of the progress of Christ's cause in the world flame with the absorbing consecration of noble and devoted womanhood. She has dared and done all for Christ. Has there been need of service? Woman has offered herself. Has there been need of testimony? Her voice has been heard at the tribunals of tyranny witnessing for her Lord. Woman's blood has stained the arena of torture and death. Woman's flesh has borne the fire, and her limbs have quivered on the rack. It has not been with any scant service or any fewness of numbers that women have confessed Christ. They have come in mighty hosts, and they have come with the courage of their convictions and with the earnestness of their sensitive nature. It has, apparently, not been as easy for women to reject Christ as it has been for men. His appeal of tenderness and love has found response in their souls. And therefore it is that the women that publish the tidings are a great host. From their very numbers great results of labor are expected of them. They form such a large proportion of the Christian Church that a large part of its work falls to them.

Moreover, there is special work which properly rests in their hands. They are the mothers and the teachers of Christian families. Our children come under their constant care. They make the first impressions upon growing minds; and those impressions are the lasting ones. They enter into the growth of the soul, just as shapes and direc-

tions that are given to the young twig are perpet-
uated and enlarged in the mature tree.   The power
of the mother is next to the power of God.   It
may help, or it may antagonize, the power of God.
At her knee the little child, given by the Creator
to her tender love, gets his first ideas of God.   Following her voice, he puts up his first mysterious
prayer to One whom he has never seen, but whose
being is certain because he is assured of it by one
whose word is the surest truth to him.   Looking
where her finger points, he sees the signals of the
divine One in flaming sun and twinkling star, in
odorous flowers and viewless winds.   And as his
feet march forward on the paths of life, her gentle
hand guides him into the rudiments of grandest
truth and into the practice of royalest virtues.
So in her wisdom is unfolded a life that shall
run into the immortalities.

Home is woman's palace.   There she reigns in
queenliest influence.   Ordering her own life in
sweet harmony to the will of Christ, she brings the
family into union with him.   Many and many
times over have I seen a whole household swayed
to subjection to our Lord by the consistent walk
and will of one maternal mind.   When in all our
homes the great host of those who hold this power
shall consecrate it to the Redeemer the golden
day of prophetic sight shall rise.

To woman, also, it is committed as a trust to

teach those who are untaught in the faith. It is characteristic of the feminine nature to put up with much self-denial for the sake of others. No one can look upon the endurance of the lowly poor in the cares of motherhood, upon the self-sacrifice of those daughters who, having been brought up in luxury, abandon all their customary privileges to become the ministers to the sick and the wounded and the perplexed, and especially to carry the gospel to the rough and wretched, to outcasts whom men despise, and to heathen whose pitiful cry for help sounds out to the Christian world, without feeling that he has come upon regal heroism, upon the grandest instances of sainthood. Death for the cause is nothing to the lives which some grand women live. You know the record which our women have made as physicians in China; carrying the medicines of healing in their left hand and the gospel of our salvation in their right hand; in the zenanas of India, entering those secluded enclosures of lonely wives and repressed daughters with the light of civilization and the cheer of feminine faith; in the groves of Ceylon, and on the forbidden soil of Japan, and in the darkness of the Dark Continent, planting schools of Christian knowledge, and seeking at least to save the children.

And here, at home, in the noon of Christian progress, how necessary is her work for the unfor-

tunate and depraved! Who can persuade like a
woman? Who can resist a voice that reminds him
of his mother's? Who can draw back from a
touch like that of the hand that soothed and ca-
ressed in the pure days that are gone? I am con-
vinced that the work of rescuing fallen men and
women from intemperance, of saving our youth
from habits of drinking, must be done by women,
a great host of whom are already enlisted for this
work; must be done by them by a method that
they have never yet tried, but which will be vastly
more effective than public talk and open conven-
tions; must be done by a hand-to-hand work, by
going in the simple earnestness of Christian faith
into all the homes of the people, and by that persuasion which woman knows best how to use,
securing a pledge from non-voters that they will
use every means in their power to overthrow the
sale of strong drink, and from voters that they will
use the ballot, irrespective of all political parties,
to outlaw the insolent rum power. When that
work can be done, well done, done in the faith of
martyr-days, the dreary curse and woes of intemperance will be among the glooms that are past.

And this principle of service, in which the special fitness of women for it stands eminently forth,
must be applied and illustrated in the parochial
work of the Church before that work will be generally consummated. That women have this special

fitness is philosophically true, and has been abundantly illustrated in the conquests and progress of Christianity. The emotional element is stronger in women than it is in men, and they are more powerfully moved by the sense of duty. One of our strong writers has said, "An ideal type, in which meekness, gentleness, patience, humility, faith and love, are the most prominent features, is not naturally male, but female." And these are the very virtues which are called for in the parochial labor of the Church. To women, very largely, must be committed the work of *teaching*. Who can seek out and gather and influence the children like them? To them, also, must be committed the *winning* to religious worship and to attention to the salvation of their souls of the vast and growing numbers who neglect God's house, know no blessed Sabbath, have no care for their souls nor for their hereafter. Who can go into all the homes, make a way for truth and light into all the hearts of lost households, gain for Christ a love that has been neglected and that has been sadly squandered in other ways, like Christ's own handmaidens? The church that is strong in women, young women and older women, who are willing to do this work, will have its hands full and its heart full, and will make Christ's heart full, too, of joy in its service and its success! The parishes are waiting for it, and the Lord is waiting for it!

It must be done on a systematized plan of Christian work. Spasmodic and promiscuous and haphazard service will not do. Each Christian worker must have an allotted and definite field, and the souls within that field, all of them, must be as familiarly known as the souls of the worker's household. The Sunday-school class is definitely bounded for each teacher. But how many teachers there are who utterly slight their work, who absolutely do nothing on plan or purpose *to save* their classes! Better, far better, never to take the place of a teacher than, taking it, to misuse it! Better not assume the care of those souls, than to have both the care and the blood of them upon your soul!

And if this work, for which women have a special fitness, cannot be done, then it were about as well to report our failure at once. We shall have no good and full account to give unless among converted and saved women there is a disposition to carry, in the love of Christ, the gospel of Christ, to the lost whom they are so well fitted to reach.

I have said that this special fitness has been abundantly illustrated in the progressive conquests of Christianity. The mothers of those great men who gave such historic grandeur to the triumph of Christianity, like the mothers of Augustine and Chrysostom, were devoted laborers for the great Master. The wives and sisters of the men who led

in the defence of the faith, and from their thrones
of power aided the cause forward, were women
who counted not their lives dear to themselves for
their love to the Redeemer.   The blood that stood
in pools on the arenas of martyrdom was blood
that flowed from the veins of maidens and mothers
who would esteem no honor so great as to live and
die for Him who died for them.   The charities of
the Church, which gave a new glory to it not only
but to our common humanity as well, were distrib-
uted by the fair hands of women, some of whom
came from palaces to tend the poor, the sick, the
dying.   There has been no age, there has been no
church, whether in dark times or in prosperous
times, that has not received new luster from the
self-denying labors and charities of Christian women, who have thus blessed the world, while they
have crowned with moral dignity themselves.

Near to the great name of Christ is the name of
the most honored of all the women of the world,
whose pure and radiant form has fixed the eyes of
all who have truly loved her Son, and has cherished a reverence which has chastened and en-
nobled the virtues which have so fitted woman for
her great part in the rescue of the race.

16

XIV

PRESENT BLESSEDNESS OF CHRISTIANS

" Blessed be the God and Father of our Lord Jesus Christ, who hath blessed us with every spiritual blessing in the heavenly places in Christ."—*Ephesians*. 1 : 3.

———

New Britain. First Church.

Much is said and much is thought of the blessedness of the saints in their future home. And thitherward our thoughts should certainly go. As the traveler, weary with sights and toils, turns longingly toward his home, as the voyager, tossed in the perils of storm and wave, gazes across the sea to his port, so should we have aspirations for the bright land that is waiting for us. But there is blessedness for the righteous this side of heaven. Our joy is not all for futurity. Our glory is not all to be revealed. There is music on the march as well as in the coming triumph. There are festivities before we come to the final feast. There is glad fellowship here like that which is to be shared hereafter. There are even some good things on this side which we cannot take over on to that side. And here and now we have *Christ*, who is the light and the glory of the heavenly world.

"Blessed be the God and Father of our Lord Jesus Christ, who hath blessed us with every spiritual blessing in the heavenly places in Christ."

This is not the tone of one who has no joy yet, who is living wholly on the expectancy of good things yet to come. "Who hath blessed us" already, not with meager gifts, but with "every spiritual blessing" as of heavenly things in Christ now.

My subject is, *The Present Blessedness of Christians.*

I. Anticipation is itself blessed. So true is this, that there is a proverb which makes anticipation more than the reality. The imagination floods the coming events with unreal light, makes them glow in deeper colors than nature ever paints. The boy who looks forward with bounding joy to vacation, finds vacation more prosy than his poetic sense had pictured it. The youth who strains on the leash of parental control in the coveting of what he fancies to be freedom, finds that freedom is a snare, and often a bondage. Men who work for competence and independence as the state of ideal bliss, sigh for the tasks of their younger and better days. The anticipation was more than the reality. In the expectation was their real happiness. Now, although this cannot be true of the looking forward to heavenly experiences, although no foretaste can equal the real enjoyment of the skies, although the eye cannot now look upon any picture which the imagination can paint so vivid as the actual scenes

of heaven, yet there is solid blessedness in the
expectation of that which is certainly to be ours,
and all the more because we know that in this
case the proverb cannot come true that our foresight shall surpass the actual vision. We are
anticipating as we sail on over these leagues of
tossing seas, through these mementoes of awful
wrecks, on these waste tracks of the mariners
who have spread their canvas before us, a haven
toward whose lighted piers prows are pointing
on every watery highway, into whose golden and
brilliant streets sweep the weary crews when their
sails are furled, to whose treasures are brought the
loaded freight from all the lands beneath the sun,
the golden crops and the costly products of till-
age and of toil. And we are not to be disappointed. Our anticipation has something substantial under it. We cannot, indeed, come up to the
reality. Wrote one who for the first time saw one
of the great epics in stone, " It was the first cathedral I had ever been in. The shock and the wonder of its grandeur took my breath away. The
vastness, coolness, stillness and splendor crushed
me,—the great solemn rays of sunlight coming in
slanting glory through the windows,—the huge
height, the impression it gave of greatness, of
pure, noble hearts, and patient, skilful hands,
toiling, but in a spirit that made the toil a holy
prayer, all was too much for me, the more so in

that while I *felt* it all, I could not analyze it. I
tried to conceal my tears." The desire of many
years found more than fulfilment. And so the
longing of all those who look forward to the
heavenly state will be more than met. The only
disappointment there, will be that of desire and
expectation *surpassed*. The greatness and the
glory, the vastness of the bliss and of the service,
will " take the breath away," will whelm the being
with delight and awe. Yet is it not a great thing
that we can anticipate that which is sure to more
than meet our fondest, fullest expectation? The
ideal will find itself surpassed by the real. So we
go on in this joyful hope and with these forepledges
our better life. We have a present blessedness in
the certainty of a greater blessedness yet to be.
Everything points forward. The gales drive us
nearer home. The pennons stream toward the
port. Every eye gazes into the distances ahead.
Our reckoning respects the time that yet remains.
Prayers go up for patience to wait. Songs that
are in all the air swell with the gladness of chorals
that are to be lifted by the redeemed of all the
nations and all the ages. There are sweet scenes
here to be looked upon and admired; but the
saints have a vision of scenes lovelier far, dimly
seen, but with glory lighting them, as, in the pictures of the old masters, in the distances of the
background will be the faint suggestion of golden

domes and aspiring pinnacles of light and white robes of spiritual beings, with flashes of glory far off too splendid for the eye to see.

The thought of these heavenly things, given to the aspirings of those who are approaching them, makes meaning for the doxology, " Blessed be the God and Father of our Lord Jesus Christ, who hath blessed us with every spiritual blessing in the heavenly places in Christ."

II. This blessedness arises from the present experiences of Christians.   It is not all in the anticipation of what they are to attain, but it is partly in the possession of what they have already gained. " Who hath blessed us with every spiritual blessing."   When we come into the adoption of children with God, so that we can truly walk in the light and love of his Fatherliness, knowing him as reconciled to us, we enter upon the enjoyment of certain great personal experiences, which are our most valued possessions ; which give us more satisfaction than anything else can give ; which remain when other things are lost ; which make us rich when we are poor, and strong when we are weak, and happy when we are miserable, and give us good company when we are lonely, and make us satisfied when we are disappointed, reversing the logic of life for us, and rendering actual that which might seem sentimental and ideal.   For when we let the true light shine on things, a new appearance

and a new value are given to them. When we get
the idea of this world as a training-school for future
study and service, it wears a different aspect from
that which it had when we made it the end in itself for our ambition and effort. When we come
to feel that our place for all eternity will depend
on our acquisitions now, that rank in heaven results from attainment on earth, we set less store
by those things which are in their nature perish-
able, and which only contribute to the gratification
of temporary senses, and we raise to a new value
those which are as immortal as ourselves, and
which will enter into the essentials of our superior
life. The gildings and frescoes of a tomb are not
of much account to that part of man which sleeps
in it. The eternal treasures of culture and power
are beyond price to that other part of man which
soars to immortality.

There are, we may say, carnal blessings,—things
which minister to the gratification of the eye and
the ear and the palate and the touch. But the eye
is to be dim to-morrow, and the ear is to catch no
sound then, and taste and touch are to be as " lost
arts" thereafter. What is it which makes of these
everything? which absorbs in these all that a
man has? which lavishes on these thought and
talent and time and wealth and wisdom? Shall a
man build on a running stream or a quicksand?
There are, too, assuredly spiritual blessings. There

are the priceless treasures of a pacified conscience
and an eternal hope and a heavenly joy. There
is pardon of sin. There is peace with God. There
is salvation. There is growth in grace. There is
adoption as children of God. There is the indwelling of the Spirit. There is the assurance of
heaven. There is sainthood which is more than
kinghood. There is childhood which is more than
princedom. There is the fact that one is redeemed
in the great love and by the great sacrifice of another, so that the darkness and the woe of sin are
past forever, and so that the serenity and the secu-
rity of eternal salvation are forever assured. These
are in the present experience of Christians. These
are the spiritual blessings with which they are now
blessed. If they do not have them it is because
they do not take them. They have the title to
them. No estate of an old family is so fortified
by records running back into antiquity, by possession through successive generations, as is the
spiritual estate of the true Christian. As the heir
looks upon his ancestral halls, as his eye takes in
the sweep of meadow and of woodland, of orchard
and of garden, he feels that they are *his* by old
inheritance, by the sure title-deeds of his ancient
family, and that no one can dispute his claim.
Here are the seals and the coat of arms and the
legend of his race and the signatures of his fathers.
He holds his property by undoubted right. So

the saint holds these great possessions now, by
royal charter, by inherited title, by the seal of divine blood, by records of the divine Spirit, by
words of inspired truth. They are his, and no
power shall separate him from them. He is in a
line of unbroken and undisputed possession. He
is in the personal enjoyment of the blessings;
knows that he has pardon and peace and salvation
and the indwelling Spirit. He is happy, or may be
happy in the fact. His own experiences, in trial,
in loss, in loneliness, in labor, in faith, lead him to
say, "Blessed be the God and Father of our Lord
Jesus Christ, who hath blessed us with every spiritual blessing in the heavenly places in Christ."

III. The present blessedness of Christians
springs from their present relation to Christ. It is
not permitted to us now to see him; the vision of
his face is future; and now we are absent from the
Lord. Yet now and here there are spiritual blessings in heavenly things in Christ. Already Christ
is more than all else. As in old galleries, where
are pictures of the great and the good there is but
one head that has *the glory* around it, distinguish-
ing him from all human persons, so in life, whatever may be our relation to those whom we esteem
and love, there is One who is altogether lovely,
whom we trust in the darkest hours, to whom we
commit all things that are most precious to us;
who abides while changes go forward, while friends

pass into the unseen, while infirmity and age lay
their burdens on us. Through distance, through
storm, through shipwreck, we see the aureola
which assures us of His presence who has said, I
will never leave thee, nor forsake thee. There is
light on every dark path, there is light on every
tempestuous sea ; it is the light of his love.

Christ has not so gone away that he has forsaken his friends. He is only absent to sight ;
but he is present to faith. He is more present
than if we could merely see him. He is humanly
away, but he is divinely with us. He speaks to
us now ; the same precious words, even with fuller
meaning, that he spake to his disciples when he
was bodily with them, are his undoubted language
to us, full of affection and sympathy. He speaks
to us in the tones that we need most to hear.
Are you in sorrow, sorrow from the loss of those
whom you could not spare, from the upsetting of
plans and hopes that you set most store by, sorrow from the immeasurable folly of those whom
you most of all wish to do well, sorrow from pain
of soul of which you can speak to no human
friend ? There is no speech that can reach you
like these full-souled words of Him who carried all
our griefs and bore all our sorrows, whose friendship is infinite, and who has the ability to do all
that his love prompts him to do. Are you in sin,
unforgiven yet, but wishing, beginning to wish,

that you may be forgiven, wanting to shake off these shackles that so hold you down and that so cramp all that is best in you? No one can speak to you like Christ; you must hear him or you *might as well be deaf to all voices.* He promises pardon and promises rest. Are you in that uncertainty that you need leadership, a hand safe enough and strong enough to guide you out of trouble into assurance and into peace and into victory at last? Well, there is but one Hand in the universe that can do it. If you have faith to grasp it and to cling to it, and still to grasp and cling, whatever betides, you will come out well. It is within your reach. It is stretched out for you. And it has been proved to be strong by the multitudes who have laid hold of it in their direst needs and with their fullest faith. Christ can do all for you as a needy sinner, as a pardoned sinner, as a sinner on the way to heaven, that he has ever done for any sinner and that you can want done for you. Look at Paul, look at John Newton, look at your precious mother, look at the most revered and the most loved and the most sanctified, and remember that their Saviour is your Saviour now, your present Saviour.

In these present relations of Christ to his people is the foundation of their present blessedness. It is well to think of what he was, it is well to think of what he forever will be; but the look back-

ward and the look forward should both be to give
us greater confidence in him now.

He is on the throne for us!   He rules the universe for us!   This work of human salvation is
so great that all the worlds should stop on their
grand revolutions before this should stop!   The
Lord Almighty, who made the world and the race
that peoples it, is the Saviour of it!   At his name
every knee shall bow, of things in heaven, and
things in earth, and things under the earth!   He
is head over all things to his Church!   If we want
safety we have it.   If we want heaven we have that.
For this union to Christ now is "heaven begun
below."   In every view, then, we may take up this
old doxology, "Blessed be the God and Father of
our Lord Jesus Christ, who hath blessed us with
every spiritual blessing in the heavenly places in
Christ."   We have an *anticipation* that cannot be
unrealized.   We have *experiences* that are full of
satisfaction.   We have *Christ* himself, the hope
of glory, the Saviour of our souls, the Friend
and Helper of our life.

In the conquests of the Mohammedans, when
Mosslemah had entered Constantinople, he would
not leave that city without the cross which hung
in its most sacred temple.   His victorious troops
had reached the gates of the city when the Greek
emperor, for that city was then a Christian city,
proposed an accommodation by the payment of

tribute and by recognizing the Mohammedan sovereignty, so that Constantinople might not fall.
But the victorious leader replied that he was under
oath that he would never depart till he had seen
the glories of Constantinople.   Accordingly he
was permitted to enter *alone*.   Outside the gates
his troops were ranged in formidable force to
carry destruction and slaughter into it if any
treachery should occur.   Within, from the gates
to the magnificent cathedral of St. Sophia, were
drawn up the splendid troops of the empire, and
between their ranks rode the solitary Mohammedan warrior.   It was a picture for a painter.
From head to foot he was clad in polished armor
of mail, but over his helmet he wore a turban of
white linen and from his shoulders down he was
covered with a mantle of finest silk.   In his bal-
dric he bore his trusty scimetar and in his hand a
lance from the head of which streamed a white
banner, the symbol of peace.   He moved silently
to the palace through the throngs who admired
his majesty and boldness.   Then, with the monarch on foot by his side, he rode to the cathedral
church.   Among all its splendid decorations there
was none like the cross of gold, so brilliant with
its jewels of untold value that it lighted the
sacred edifice.   On this he laid his hands, swear-
ing that he would never leave the city without it.
Fixing it, reversed, to the head of his lance, by

the white symbol of peace, he bore it in triumph through the streets of the insulted city, just as his army was about to enter it to avenge his supposed death. The cross was the sole spoil which Constantinople yielded to its imperious invader. With that in his possession he was satisfied to leave all its other treasures behind him. Without that he would have called his eager armies within the gates and wasted the wealth and glory of that great metropolis.

To us it is offered, with all that it means, in peaceful and welcome possession. We have not to gain it by conquest, but by willing acceptance.

Not only the cross, but He who gave it its meaning and glory, are within our reach, are urged upon our loving reception. Christ and his cross! These are ours now—possessions above all others, our present joy and our eternal glory. With these, we may renounce all other treasures. Without these, nothing—not the wealth of the world, not the honors, nor the proudest successes of the world—could satisfy us.

My brethren, with us let Christ be *first*; let Christ be *all*.

17

XV

UNTARNISHED DISCIPLESHIP

" Will ye lie among the sheepfolds, as the wings of a dove covered with silver, and her pinions with yellow gold."— *Psalms* 68 : 13.

———

NORTH CHURCH, NEW HAVEN.

Also in *Treasury*, New York.

UNTARNISHED DISCIPLESHIP

The doves of God, flashing with their plumage
of silver and of gold, above the earth, while yet of
it, are the significant emblems of those who are
aspiring to the renewed life. The greater the
light is in which they soar, the greater is the
beauty reflected on feather and pinion. The
stronger the gale is against which they sweep, the
quicker will be the flash of light from beating wing
and quivering plume. Above all foulness and all
deadly miasms, above the low-settling mists and
the entangling nets and the destructive shots of
the fowler, they mount into the unobstructed fields
of the firmament and, from the glorious vision-
place of the upper air, look down on the dimmed
and fouled world beneath them.

It is the symbol of saints overcoming and aspiring. It matters but little what interpretation we
give to the obscure opening clause of the text,
whether we read as in the old version, among the
pots of the kitchen, with their defiling crock and
smut, or among the hurdles, or among the sheep-

folds, or within the boundaries, all of which meanings have been given to it. Nor does it matter much
whether we make the wings of the dove refer
directly to the people of God, as when the Psalm-
ist speaks of " the soul of thy turtledove " in his
prayer to God, or as when the Prophet speaks of
them as " trembling as a bird out of Egypt, and as
a dove out of the land of Assyria; " or whether
we consider this as a description of the opulent
spoil which should inflame the world-conquerors,
and should rebuke those who lie at ease without a
struggle to gain it; or whether it is the promise
and figure of the brilliant lot appointed to victorious believers in the lap of coming peace; all of
which meanings have been gathered from it.

Whether *now*, living amidst the corruptions of a
world with which they are at war, they keep clear
of its defilements and soar above its degradations
as on the wings of doves flashing in the sunlight
with silver and with gold; or whether *hereafter*,
all the struggle and the sorrow past, as those who
have returned from battle to their homes in peace,
they will be adorned with jewels of immortal splendor, like a dove with wings of silver and pinions
of gold; in either case it brings before us in brilliant figure the disciples of Christ untarnished by
the world and prepared for the purity of the
heavenly state. Perhaps the meaning which St.
Cyril gave it a millennium and a half ago is as

good as any: "They will no longer mind earthly
things, but mount up to heaven as on the wings
of the divine dove." So it harmonizes with that
other Scripture in the same Book, "Blessed are
they that are perfect in the way, who walk in the
law of the Lord;" and with that characterization
which an apostle gives of "pure religion and undefiled before our God and Father," as "to keep
himself unspotted from the world."

That we who would serve God and follow Christ
are *in the world* is a palpable condition of that
service and following. Christ himself would not
pray that we should be taken out of the world, but
that his Father would keep us from the evil that is
in it. For the discipline from which comes highest character, life in this world is well adapted.
There might be flabby sentiment and pusillani-
mous purpose and feeble faith under conditions of
ease and carelessness, and that involved no struggling. But it is better to have some risk and even
some failures, than to have dead uniformity and
unmitigated mediocrity, if out of the whole trial
shall proceed strong and enduring character that
shall fit those who have it not only for honor but
for eternal service, so that they shall mount up
with wings as eagles, and run and not be weary,
and walk and not faint.

That the world, separated from God, given over
to the corruptions of sin, whether considered as

made up of the men who know nothing else but
to serve it, or of the enticements which it holds
out to lust in many ways, is to Christians *a source
of constant defilement*, is simply a matter of on-
going history and unwritten biography. Its temptations are continual and perpetual, and those who
ought to soar like doves on gleaming wings of
speed and strength, lie like scullions among sooty
pots.   Those who are "called to be saints" and
are washed with the water of regeneration, are
defiled with the impurities of ungodliness, so that
the hands which should be clean are fouled, and
the souls that should be cleansed are like the
nests of unclean birds.   The life in the world is
full of risk and disaster; many who appear well for
a time are overthrown to their dishonor and to the
discredit of the Church.   So the ecclesiastical records have on them names that are smirched, names
that would be worthless on a promissory note, and
would carry no weight as an endorsement on business paper.

That real Christians, though in the world and
though exposed to the polluting enticements of it,
should *live above it and as not of it*, like doves
that have their home and get their living on it, yet
breathe the pure air on high, and spread their
shining wings in flights toward the sky, is the
plainest duty of their heavenly calling and their
holy profession.   It is not for them to wear the

grime of the sheepfolds, though they lie among them, to get the contamination of sin, though their business is in the midst of it, to fall into the polluted habits of sinners, though necessarily in their society. Every Christian should be like a shining light in the midst of darkness; like a precious gem in the refuse and rubbish of the mine; like salt in the corrupting and spoiling masses. He should come forth from all the world's affairs in which he must be engaged, from its business and its politics and its society, with a character untarnished, a mind clean and heavenly, a person pure, a conscience unseared, his whole individuality free from contamination, as out of the crock and soot of pots sails the dove with her wings covered with silver and her feathers with yellow gold.

The Christian faith demands this incorruptibleness by reason of *the supreme purity of its Founder*. That divine life, which appeared in human garb, subject to the conditions of our real life, yet maintaining evermore its heavenly quality, making one path of light through the environing darkness of the world, is a model and an example for all who profess to follow if. He knew no sin. He was indeed touched with the feeling of our infirmities, yet it was without the stain or smirch or distress of sin. He was holy, harmless, undefiled, separate from sinners, and, though on the earth, made higher than the heavens.

He did no sin, neither was guile found in his
mouth.   Righteousness was the girdle of his loins,
and faithfulness the girdle of his reins.   He
suffered for us, leaving us an example that we
should follow his steps.   And that example is the
brightest thing in all history.   It is the only pure
light in the darkness of a world that would be
all night without it.   It has worked on men in
these later centuries of the Christian dispensation
with the same power that it had on the disciples in
the earlier centuries.   It has inspired the noblest
life among men of culture and taste and high position, even as it has dignified the lowly life of the
poor and ignorant and overworked, blessing the
castle as it has blessed the cottage beside it, making
Christian faith the richest possession of the scholar
and the statesman, as of the street-sweeper and the
washerwoman.   We know what grace it has added
to learning, and to the manliest accomplishments,
and what a leading force it has been in the progress of the Christian civilizations and the world's
later enlightenment.   It has also worked downward
into the lowest strata of society and brought up,
with its quickening forces, large enrichment from
the otherwise degraded elements of humanity, as
from deep and dark mines the richest jewels are
quarried for sword-hilts and crowns.   In his " History of European Morals," Lecky observes, "It is
the peculiarity of the Christian types that, while

they have fascinated the imagination, they have
also purified the heart. The tender, winning, and
almost feminine beauty of the Christian Founder,
the Virgin Mother, the agonies of Gethsemane and
Calvary, the many scenes of compassion and suffering that fill the sacred writings, are the pictures
which, for eighteen hundred years, have governed
the imaginations of the rudest and most ignorant
of mankind. Associated with the fondest recol-
lections of childhood, with the music of the church
bells, with the clustered lights and tinsel splendor
that seem to the peasant the very ideal of majesty;
painted over the altar where he received the companion of his life, around the cemetery where so
many whom he had loved were laid, on the sta-
tions of the mountain, on the portal of the vine-
yard, on the chapel where the storm-tossed mariner fulfills his grateful vow; keeping guard over
his cottage door, looking down upon his humble
bed, forms of tender beauty and gentle pathos forever haunt the poor man's fancy, and silently win
their way into the very depths of his being."

And thus it comes to pass that throughout the
peoples to whom Christ is the one living Example,
and on whose lives he has wrought as the one
object of an undoubting faith, for whom they can
live, for whom equally they can die, there is developed a character of strength and purity and
incorruptibleness, which would grace and dignify

any annals. Out of black mines, out of the smoke and soot of furnaces and forges, out of the slime and ooze of mud-flats and tan-vats, out of the dust and grime of mills and engines, out of the close air of the forecastle and the soil of plantations, has come the clean character of those who were there, walking with the immaculate Redeemer, and aspiring to the heavenly life, as from the soot of pots doves might soar with wings covered with silver and feathers with yellow gold.

It shows the might of the Saviour's power, the influence of his supreme purity. That which came upon him during the prayer which he offered when he was being baptized—when "the Holy Ghost descended in a bodily form, as a dove, upon him, and a voice came out of heaven, 'Thou art my beloved Son; in thee I am well pleased'"—has come upon those who have taken him as their one Saviour and Example, and they have felt his renewing power and his sanctifying grace, purging them of foulness and viciousness, and giving them ability to walk in newness of life. The Holy Spirit has created in them a clean heart, and has renewed a right spirit within them, so that they have put off the old man, which is corrupt, according to the deceitful lust, and have put on the new man, which, after God, is created in righteousness and true holiness. And thus they have been brought into oneness with the Son of

God, " for as many as are led by the Spirit of God,
these are the sons of God."

The Christian life is a simple following of Christ.
The standard which we need to hold before us is
Christ himself.

Again, the Christian faith demands that believers should be undefiled in the world by reason of
the pureness of the early Christians. To this
they were enjoined by the Apostolic writings, as
they were stimulated to it by the Apostolic example.   Amidst the open and abounding corruptions
of the pagan world they maintained a pure deportment and conversation, which was a rebuke to
their enemies, as it was a renown to themselves.
It was a standing and an irresistible and unanswer-
able testimony to the superiority of their faith over
whatever tenets of pagan belief.   Their conversation was in heaven.   Though in the world, though
exposed to peculiar and great hardships as followers of Christ, they proved that their thoughts and
their love went to One who had died for them, but
now reigned for them.   They were exposed to the
hardest trials, to persecutions, to death.   They
had but one answer.   They were Christians in life,
in death as well.   One who was threatened with
torments without mercy, if he did not renounce
Christ, replied : " There is nothing which we more
earnestly desire than to endure torments for the
sake of our Lord Jesus Christ."   And one •of the

noblest of the martyrs, while his hands were bound
behind him at the stake, and the fagots were piled
around him for the fire, prayed: "Omnipotent
Lord God, Father of thy beloved and blessed
Son, Jesus Christ, through whom we have received
the knowledge of Thee, I bless Thee that on this
day and hour Thou hast counted me worthy to
make one of the number of thy martyrs, to partake of the cross of Christ, and to look for the resurrection to eternal life, both of soul and body,
through the power of the Holy Spirit, praying
that I may be received to-day among the number
of thy saints as a rich and acceptable sacrifice."

About ten years after the death of St. John, the
younger Pliny became a Roman proconsul in a
region where the Christians were numerous. He
wrote to the Emperor Trajan for instructions as to
the treatment of the professors of Christianity.
He says that he could collect nothing against
them except what he regarded as "a depraved
and excessive superstition." And, as he described it, their religion was that "they were
accustomed, on a stated day, to meet before day-
light, and to repeat among themselves a hymn to
Christ as to a god, and to bind themselves, with
an oath, by an obligation of not committing any
wickedness; also of not violating their promise,
or denying a pledge; after which it was their custom to separate and to meet again at a harmless

meal." The strong writer from whom I have once quoted, says: "The fathers were long able to challenge their adversaries to produce a single instance in which any other crime than his faith was proved against a martyr, and they urged with a just and noble pride, that whatever doubt there might be of the truth of the Christian doctrines, or of the divine origin of the Christian miracles, there was, at least, no doubt that Christianity had transformed the characters of multitudes, vivified the cold heart by new enthusiasm, redeemed, regenerated and emancipated the most depraved of man-kind. Noble lives, crowned by heroic deaths, were the best arguments of the infant Church." The Christianity which commenced with this separateness from the world's defilement, and stood by it against the terrors of indignity and death, should be maintained to the end, as above reproach, and free from contamination. In the early and dark days *a dove* was represented as issuing from the mouth of dying Christians, and winging his swift flight to light and glory inexpressible. The later Church caught the meaning of the beautiful symbol of the earlier Church and transfigured it!

Also, the Christian faith calls for undefiled deportment and character in its professors in the world, in virtue of *the immaculate purity of the world to which they aspire*. They desire a better country, that is, a heavenly. Their Lord has gone to prepare a place for them; and he will receive them unto himself, that where he is they may be also. And they shall see his face, and shall behold his glory, and shall be like him, and shall be presented faultless before the presence of his glory with exceeding joy, and shall shine forth as the sun in the kingdom of their Father.

It is that a people may be prepared here for the pure world of light and glory that Christ's great work was done. He gave himself for it, that he might sanctify and cleanse it with the washing of water by the Word, that he might present it to himself a glorious Church, not having spot or wrinkle, or any such thing, but that it should be holy and without blemish. His redeemed will ascribe glory and dominion unto him, who loved them and washed them from their sins in his own blood, and made them kings and priests unto God. They are forever to possess an inheritance incorruptible and undefiled and that fadeth not away.

And it is clearly stated, as a warning against the intrusion of the polluted, that there shall in nowise enter into it anything that defileth, neither whatsoever worketh abomination or a lie. The pure in heart shall see God. Those who see his face will see it in righteousness and in incorruption.

Now they are in a world that is soiled by sin.
They cannot touch it, with longing or with lust,
without bearing away the foul marks of its grime,
without knowing that the smutch of its pollution
dishonors their calling. The temptations abound.
The appeal is made to imperious passions, to the
downward proclivities of a fallen, inherited nature;
sometimes to habits that were formed before the
renewal by the Spirit, sometimes to desires that
are good in themselves and wrong only in their
abuse. It is most easy to have the fine gold of
the Christian profession tarnished, and the silver
speech of sainthood sullied. Many and many
come up from the world's ways contaminated,
the beauty and glory of their vocation gone. But
there is another world that draws us. Eye cannot,
indeed, see it; but we know that it shines on high,
and that the path on which we should walk leads
straight to its gates of pearl. The victorious
saints, washed and made clean, wear their white
robes within its walls, and the purest music of
golden harps floats through its open doors. There
Christ, the heavenly Lamb, leads his redeemed
into pure fields and beside clear waters. No stain
of sin is ever there. No defilement tarnishes the
character of any who are privileged to enter.
They go on, they grow and mature, in the excellence and brilliance of an unsullied life, of an
immortal angelhood. Here then and now and

18

evermore, hold to your high calling. Let your conversation be in heaven. As you are journeying toward it, be filled with the spirit of it, and let your lives resemble the lives of those who are now what you hope soon to be.

XVI

THE DESIRE TO SEE JESUS

" Sir, we would see Jesus."—*John* 12 :21.

———

Second Church, Germantown, Pa.

Certain Greeks were among the multitudes who from many lands had come up to Jerusalem to participate in the great festival of the Hebrew nation. From what place they had come we are not told. The Greeks were full of enterprise; they were the merchants of the world. There is a tradition that they were a deputation sent by King Abgarus of Edessa to invite the Messiah to an asylum in his dominions. They were probably from some remote city, for if they had been dwellers in the land of Israel they would have had earlier opportunity to see the Lord. We do not know the object or purpose they entertained in seeking the interview. Nor have we any further account of them. But their desire to see Jesus at this time was a fact of great significance in its bearing on the kingdom of the Lord. He was near the crisis of his work. The hour, the decisive hour, for which all the ages had waited, for which the world had existed, was at hand. Everything dearest to man hung on the result of that fateful hour. Christ was greatly moved by it. His whole nature shrank from the crushing burden that he was to bear. On him were to be laid the iniquities of us all. He was to carry the sins of the world. In his own person he was to be wounded for the transgressions of mankind.

Then, his people, those to whom he first came, were rejecting him, were despising his claims, were plotting for his death. At that time appeared on the scene these Greeks from some other land, who, perhaps, had never heard of Christ until within the few days preceding, who had witnessed, it may be, the triumphant entry of this remarkable person into Jerusalem, and heard the voices of loyal love and royal greeting which had welcomed him, now asking in courteous language, with modest yet firm request, that they might see Jesus.

It was a request remarkable in itself, and remarkable as occurring at that juncture. It indicated coming history. It was a recompense for the guilty rejection of Christ by the Jews. It was the first fruits of the Gentile world. It was the beginning of the fulfilment of prophecy. "Nations shall come to thy light, and kings to the brightness of thy rising. . . . they all gather themselves together, they come to thee: thy sons shall come from far, . . . the wealth of the nations shall come unto thee." The glowing visions which had thrilled in the imagery of the Hebrew seers were coming to fulfilment. Already, before he was lifted up, he was beginning to. draw all men unto him. The other sheep which were not of the Jewish fold were beginning to hear his voice, and were coming to the one fold. He was not to give his life, as had been prophetically said, for that nation only, but that he might also gather together into one the children of God that are scattered abroad. These Greeks were the forerunners of the unnumbered multitudes which, from peoples outside of the old economy, were to give Christ satisfaction for the work which he was to do.

All along there had been recruits to the kingdom from the uncovenanted peoples; men who in the midst of surrounding darkness groped their way to the true light. For " There was the true light, even the light which lighteth every man, coming into the world; " every man, wherever he may live, on lonely islands of the mid-sea, in the dense forests of the Dark Continent, in the slums of enlightened cities, all these have light by which they might walk in the sonship of God if they did not love darkness rather than light. " For the invisible things of him since the creation of the world are clearly seen, being perceived through the things that are made, even his everlasting power and divinity; that they may be without excuse." Men, everywhere, are without excuse for their sins, for not loving God. And they know it. Other men may try to excuse them, but their own consciences accuse them.

We have no record of many who probably have followed the light which they had; but the names of a few suggest many more, and from time to time we hear of others, enough to imply that out of the unevangelized world Christ may gain trophies even from peoples whose general characteristics are low and depraved. We have the account of Melchisedek and Job and Jethro and Ruth and Hiram and the Queen of Sheba and Naaman; of three centurions of the Roman army, the centurion of Capernaum, the centurion at the cross, the Centurion Cornelius; of Lydia; of the Ethiopian eunuch; of Zacchæus. Of one of these our Lord said, " I have not found so great faith, no, not in Israel." And then we have that remarkable statement: " And I say unto you, that many shall come from the east and the west, and shall sit down with Abraham, and Isaac, and Jacob, in the kingdom of heaven: but the sons of the kingdom shall be cast forth into the outer darkness." And so it may still be true that from heathen lands some shall follow the dim light they have and be conducted by it to heaven, while those who have the privileges of the gospel land shall reject their bright light and be cast into outer darkness.

As the wise men came from the east to the cradle of the Saviour, so these Greeks came from

the west to his cross. They were the beginnings
of the fulfilment of prophecy, that unto him shall
the obedience of the peoples be, and that the desir-
able things of all nations shall come unto him.
Christ saw in it the renewal, yes, the sign of the
fulfilment of the prophecy of his kingdom, which
was to be a world kingdom and to include all
nations and tongues and peoples.

Some things of importance are brought to mind
by this occurrence. These Greeks *cherished the
convictions* which had been stirred in them respect-
ing Christ. Possibly they had heard rumors of
him in their own land. The fact that a wonderful
worker had appeared in Israel had gone forth
among the nations. Rumor flies on unseen wings.
It goes as if on the rays of morning light. It per-
meates peoples widely scattered. You hear of it in
unexpected places. It generally enlarges as it
goes. St. Luke tells us that " this report went forth
concerning him in the whole of Judæa, and all the
region round about." No doubt it spread into other
and remoter regions. Merchants carried it. Soldiers and sailors, escort of caravans, travelers, carried it. Men who met on other business spoke of
it to one another, as we speak of the inauguration
of a president, or any other great event that is in
popular thought. Perhaps, as we have intimated,
they saw the demonstration the day before, when
Christ came into the city from the Mount of Olives,

with a great escort, and with hosannas and rejoic-
ings of the people of all ages, who saluted him as
the King of Israel.   They may have been among
those who asked, Who is this? and heard the reply,
This is the prophet, Jesus, from Nazareth of Gali-
lee.   At all events, they had convictions that they
ought to see him and to hear him.   These convictions they cherished.

This is where many men are weak.   They allow
convictions that they have to be lost.   They are
impressed by what they hear of the Saviour, of
his work for others, of his cure of blind men, of
sick men, of his raising to life of dead men.   They
hear the testimony of converted men.   They see
the new lives of neighbors and friends who have
seen Jesus and who are walking with him.   They
learn from the Scriptures, and from the preaching,
of the sacrifice of Christ for them, of the way of
salvation and acceptance by repentance and faith
and obedience.   Events are all the time occurring
in the community, in their own circle, possibly in
their own family, which excite them with the warning they give, and speak forth, as if it were a personal word, Prepare for what must come to you!
prepare to meet thy God!   Roused by all this,
quickened to a sense of duty, they should cherish
their convictions, deepen the lessons and impressions they have received.   But instead of that, they
pay little attention to them: they turn to other

affairs: they occupy themselves with things which inevitably dissipate seriousness. If they were to cherish the impressions which they receive from truth, from providence, from the Holy Spirit, they might enter on a new life. Such cherished impressions would lead on to still deeper ones. They would be God's agency for salvation. They would grow into the irrepressible longing to see Jesus and to learn of him and to become his followers. This is the way that divine life comes to men dead in trespasses and sins. They must do something. • They are not to be passive. They are not to say, with folly, that they are waiting God's time, that if they are to be saved they shall be saved, that some other season will be more convenient. *That* is the way to destroy all good feelings, all desires for God, all hope of conversion. Men have many good opportunities to be saved; they do not improve them. They throw them away. Instead of saying, This is God's leading, and I must improve and use it and make the most of it, they banish the sentiment, and rush into business or study or frivolity. And so many occasions of conversion pass, and many souls lose the prize which is offered them, which is placed within their reach, which might easily have been theirs forever.

Those certain Greeks *used the means* which were necessary. They saw Philip, who had a Greek name, and they applied to him. They asked in a winning and respectful way, in the courteous manner of the Greeks, who were the French of the ancient world, for an introduction to this great Rabbi. " Sir, we would see Jesus," they said. Philip, pleased with their manner and their desire, immediately told Andrew, and Andrew and Philip at once sought the Master and told him, and the Master undoubtedly promptly received them, and made his address bear upon their case, for their help and conversion. They sought to see Jesus through the disciples. They consulted those who knew him. They did not go to his enemies for counsel. They took advice of his friends. They did not stand aloof and say, " Perhaps he will pass this way and give us an opportunity to speak to him." They did not say, "We have nothing to do about it. It is not our concern." They did not treat the matter with indifference, with neglect, with aversion ; but they took hold of it for themselves ; they came to Philip and asked him, showing that they were in earnest, and that they wanted to make the acquaintance of Christ. This is where too many fail. They go to philosophizing about the subject, or they try to evade responsibility, or they shirk their own duty. They do not use the means they have, which God puts into their hands. They do not hold themselves to the personal task of doing what is necessary to be done.

Everywhere else they dote on their free agency ;

only here they would disown it. It is God's work, they say. Yes, it is God's work, exactly as the harvest is God s work. But the farmer plows and enriches and cultivates the ground, and then the harvest ripens and he gathers it. It is God's harvest. But the man used the means to get it. Conversion is God's harvest. As Christ looked on the unconverted multitudes he said, "The harvest is white!" The souls were there that needed saving. If you would be converted you must do as the farmer does to get his harvest. You must search the Scriptures. They teach of Christ, and if you follow their instructions you will be saved. You must seek Christians, the ministers of Christ, the friends of Christ. It is their business and their joy to help you. You must pray. You must go to Christ. You must do all that you can do. You must feel that nothing is done till all is done. You must seek until you find. You must knock until the door of salvation is opened. You must ask until the gracious and full and blessed answer comes from God.

One man uses the means and he is saved. Another man refuses to use them, and he is lost. There is nothing strange about it. One man uses the means for harvest; his garners are full. Another man refuses to use them; he starves. Here is no mystery. Carry into this thing, my friends, the sense that you use in inferior things;

act as you act about your worldly occupations, and you will have similar results. *There never was yet a man who fairly and fully used the means for his own conversion who was not converted!* The responsibility lies on the man. *God offers all the help that any soul needs and all, too, that God wisely can give.* He has never said to any child of Adam, Seek you me in vain! That is not God. For he would have all men to be saved. And he has provided the sufficient means and made the sufficient promises and now waits for sinners to use them.

The Greeks *availed themselves of what was then at hand.* They put the right meaning into the little word *now.* They did not make it mean any time, nor some time. They did not say, We will send home and get a letter of introduction to him, written in Greek. They saw Philip, and they applied to him, right then and there. Men say, I am not prepared yet. I am not good enough. I will wait for the evangelist. I will wait for the revival. I am too young! I don't understand some things. I will study up. I will consult books and doctors. You want to avail yourself of what is now at hand. You can't afford to take any risk. You know nothing about to-morrow. This night thy soul may be required of thee. The next storm may burst on your dwelling. You need the Rock.

The Greeks might have said, When we come up to the next feast, we will see Jesus. Ah! before that the Christ was betrayed and crucified; Gethsemane was on the next day but one, and Calvary was the day after that, and all was over! Before the time that you are thinking of, your death may come, your opportunity be gone, your fate be determined.

The Greeks learned that it was *not enough to see Christ*; they must serve him. The Christian life consists in obedience. Repentance respects what is past; faith respects the present; obedience is for all the future. And obedience is the proof of repentance and faith and love. It demonstrates friendship. It is the test of loyalty.

The Greeks, by their coming, brought *great comfort to Christ*. He said, Now is my soul troubled. It was the hour of darkness. He was anticipating the dreadful experiences that were at hand. Then, on that sense of woe, came before him these strangers, representatives of the great Gentile world, the vast nations outside of Judaism, who were to be redeemed by what he should suffer. He saw of the travail of his soul, and was satisfied. For this cause came I unto this hour, he said. So he was comforted and strengthened. The glorious result filled his vision. It overpassed the means by which it was to be achieved. I, if I be lifted up from the earth, will draw all men

unto myself, he said, signifying by what manner of
death he should die.   I came to save the world,
he said.   The Greeks lightened the load, because
it fills the Redeemer with joy to know that his
death will not be in vain.   Would you give joy
and comfort to Christ?   When his angels in
heaven rejoice over one sinner who repenteth, he
rejoices with them.

Those Greeks *voiced the want of the world.*
The universal longing, if it could come to expression, would be, We would see Jesus!   He only
can satisfy human souls.   He only can meet the
deepest need of every one of you.   Those inquiring Greeks had not the Jewish advantages; but
they went into the kingdom before the Pharisees.
While the favored Jews were rejecting him, the
earnest Greeks were seeking him.   So, to-day, the
heathen are before you.   With all your light you
are left; in all their darkness they are finding the
true Light.   There are more conversions among
our missionary churches than in the churches at
home.   Islanders of the sea, natives of India and
Japan, are entering into the kingdom of heaven
before you.

But if you would not now see Jesus, let it be
remembered that you *will one day see him.*   "Behold, he cometh with the clouds; and every eye
shall see him, and they which pierced him."   They
who pierced him on the cross, they who wounded

him afresh by rejecting his love, all shall see him. Now, you might seek and see him to your advantage. Then, you will only see him, if you remain his enemies, to your confusion and anguish.

With words full of pathos and tenderness, even as he spoke to the Greeks in his last public discourse, would he now speak to you, giving you divine welcome to his love and service.

A few months ago, we, in New England, were thrilled by the proud welcome which you in Philadelphia gave to the brave captain of the steamship *Missouri* when that ship moved up your river to her pier. Off from the sinking *Danmark*, and out from the risks of the deep sea, he brought the imperiled men to your fair and hospitable city. You honored yourselves when you honored him, and the echoes of your cheers were in all the air of our great land. My friends in this church, it falls to your lot and privilege to be the rescuers of imperiled souls, who, whether they speak it aloud or not, would see Jesus. And be sure of this, that the city of God will greet you with celestial ovation, if, as Philip and Andrew conducted the inquiring Greeks to Christ, you lead these, your friends and neighbors, to see the love of the Master and to go with you over the dangerous sea, on which we sail to the haven of eternal peace!

19

XVII

LIGHT AT EVENING

"It shall come to pass. that at evening time there shall be light."—*Zechariah* 14 : 7.

———

GRAND AVENUE CHURCH. NEW HAVEN.

LIGHT AT EVENING

Religion reverses the order of nature. Religion is revolution. It overthrows the old dynamics. It changes the current of affairs. It introduces new principles, new motives, new hopes, new powers even, inspires with new ambitions, reveals a new world, as the telescopic lenses open the pathway for sight into mystic spaces which had been as a formless blank and roll into view mighty orbs of brilliance and motion and density. It makes that light which had before been dark, so that this old prediction comes true, that at evening time it shall be light.

Evening is the sober close of day. The shadows lie long on the earth and belt it with their bands of gloom. The beams of sunshine that had glowed on the landscape begin to flame up the sky in crimson and gold; horizon reflects from horizon; and the firmament glows with the pomp of an evening glory that surpasses the radiance of noon. We have but to imagine this as prolonged, as in the northern latitudes, where golden light shimmers on cold floes and bergs of ice and the

desolation of wintry seas, to have a night that
shall know no darkness, where the night shall be
as the day, and the day shall be prolonged to the
morning.   It shall come to pass that at evening
time it shall be light.

First, there is the *light of home* that shines at
each day's evening upon the reunited family.
The day calls to toil, to separation, to diverse
duties.   The father goes forth to business and
devotes himself to that, that he may provide for
those who are as his own life to him.   The
mother busies herself with the thousand cares
that must ever be repeated to make the home the
place of rest and comfort and joy, that it may be a
place of neatness and sweetness and attractiveness,
that it may be a still harbor after the winds and
storms and seas, and, it may be, wrecks, of the
turbulent day.   The children have been at school
or at labor that they may contribute to the common support, and, wearied, vexed with the colli-
sions and corrosions of the busy day, they come
within the magnetism of parental love and forget
the heartburnings of the outside world in the
peace and freedom of family life.   The occur-
rences of the day pass in review, and things that
were hard and abusive and that wrenched the
fibers of the finer feelings, dissolve in the alembic
of love that contains perfect confidence, the protection of fatherhood, the tenderness of mother-

hood, the trust of childhood. Through the day
they are all parted, but the evening brings them
together and kindles a light that makes the hearth-
stone bright and illumines the dwelling. In Philadelphia the houses have dark shutters, and at
evening they are closed.* When the gas is
lighted, and the rooms blaze with brilliance, and
the family is assembled, and the music begins, and
there is the cheer of home and forgetfulness of the
outside noise and competition, the houses look
dark and forbidding to the passer-by; but those
who are within, singing the songs of the children
of the Kingdom, reading in the lore of laureated
writers, getting inspiration from pictures and
books and the experiences of human life, realize
that there is no place like that, and though the
streets may be dark and the marts of business may
be deserted, in the companionship and confidence
of home is reached the fulfilment of the saying
that at evening time it shall be light.

In old English homes, where the wainscotings
bear the tracery of a thousand years ago, where
the family life is enriched by the traditions that
have filtered through the memories of many generations, I have found the same light, softened in the
haze of antiquity, but making gladsome each
evening after the toil of the day was done, in the
reunion of those who had been parted and in the

*In late years a custom honored in its breach.

quiet enjoyment of one another.   And in German
homes, on the banks of the Neckar and in the
charming city of Munich, the same light has
greeted me; and so on, wherever our Christianity lightens the home and the family, it must
be that when the tasks of the fretted day are over
the toilers come together to find that at evening
time it shall be light.

Secondly, there will be the *light of redemption*
in the evening of the world's history.   Redemption is delayed.   The morning of humanity has
been long and sad and full of hard and bitter experience.   There came the strange Fall, breaking the
promise of the race, breaking the crown that sat
so regally on the head of man.   Then came the
experiment of apostasy; with blood shed in crime,
and blood shed in expiation; with battle-fields and
altar-groves; with man's red right hand turned
against his fellow man, and banners of brothers
flaunting defiance and hostility; with oppression
and ignorance and scorn, with repentance and
alleviation and missions of charity: a mingled,
blurred record, pages of whiteness alternating
with pages soiled and black: a gloomy morning,
as when sunrise is back of heavy clouds that will
not lift from the horizon, and storm-sheets sweep
through the murky atmosphere, and the light of
day is almost blotted out.   Six thousand years
this morning has numbered.   And yet the signs

of noon are scant and slow. It will be a long day
for the race to live out It will cost many sacrifices before heathendom will be all reclaimed.
There must be costly offerings to save this self-
destroyed race. You think that there is light here
and now. Yes, light! but the shadows that crowd
it! Crimes, prisons, executions; broken hearts
of mothers and sisters; pitiful weakness of men
who misuse all their powers; tendencies backward
to barbarism; drunkenness, chief crime and leader
of crimes; this nation of ours, a nation of light,
you say, spending six millions annually for Christian missions, but spending seven hundred millions
for intoxicating drinks. Do you look for noon
yet? Noon is light. The sun pours its floods
then from the zenith. Not yet can it be noon.
We might faint but for the promise, that God is
light, and in him is no darkness at all. He will
make his light to shine, and all the world will be
flooded and warmed and kindled by it.

But it will come later on. It will come at evening. There must be slow, great changes. Great
histories must be written first. Great expenditures
must be made. Great, good lives of God's children must be offered. But by and by, in the
Lord's own time, the redemption will come, the
nations will be saved. Then, in the full radiance
of Christ's completed work, it shall be seen that at
evening time it shall be light.

Thirdly, there will be the light of *divine consolation* in the midst of human discouragement. It is a hard task to work up the human elements of the divine kingdom. You are met by old follies, hardened habits, bitter prejudices, and, what is worse than all, the cool indifference that has neither reason nor purpose back of it. These are the "chariots of iron" that bar all progress and prevent all victory. They stand in solid and threatening array across the path of the kingdom, and keep back those who would enter in. You present the gospel plainly, you gain the approval of the conscience and carry the judgment, and yet you find the same obstinacy of will, the same perversion of conduct, the same continuance in the old way, the same refusal of obedience, the same aloofness from Christ. The influence which might be given to the righteous cause, which would turn the scales in favor of the weightiest matter, which would give momentum and power to the truth, is refused, contrary to a wise prudence and the best interests of society. You can get no right answer from those who most need to give it. You can get no committal for Christ from those who control most precious interests which should be secured for him. Worse: you find Christians, at least professed Christians, whom you have worked for, in whose evident progress you have taken delight, on whom you have leaned for help

and comfort, swinging away from duty, as ships
swing from moorings in the stress of storm, turning their back on privileges and ordinances, ex-
hibiting a disposition which is a dishonor to the
Christian profession, and hindering the work
which needs their consecration and consistency.
In all this are the elements of profound discouragement. You would naturally despair of the righteous cause. You would conclude that there is no
use of further effort, it is certain that all endeavor
will be balked. But out of the gloom comes the
cheer of divine consolation. You see the foot-
marks of One who was despised and rejected of
men, who had no beauty that the race desired,
who was buffeted and crucified, and who bought
the world only with blood. And so in the pity of
Christ, in the sorrowful forbearance of the Son of
God, you get the lessons of serenest consolation,
and in the evening of your discouragement there
shall be light.

Fourthly, there will be light *for the sinful soul*
in the darkness of its conviction. It is a depress-
ing revelation that comes before an awakened sinner. In his blindness and stupor he was accustomed to think that all was well; that he was not
very far out of the way; that he had not done anything very wrong; that his accountability was a
slight matter, and that God would not find much
in him to condemn. But the awakening changes

all this. It takes away all self-justification. It
sweeps off all personal reliances. It discloses a
situation of unexpected peril. A flash of lightning at sea has flamed on the side of an iceberg,
and crew and passengers have had disclosed to
them the danger that their ship would be instantly
crushed. A lamp was brought to a party that
had groped in a dark cave, and they found that
they had paused on the brink of a yawning chasm,
over which another step would have precipitated
them. The lightning and the lamp created no
danger; they only revealed that which existed.
The conviction of sin creates no danger to the
soul; it only makes evident that which before existed. But it is vastly important both to know and
to realize the facts. For then the way of escape will
be sought. And when that is sought CHRIST, in
the fullness of his mediation and in the generosity
of his offers, will be apprehended; so that in the
solemn sorrow of the soul, in the twilight of its
self-reproach and of its wonder if there can be
escape, He will be revealed a full Deliverer, so
that at evening time it shall be light.

Fifthly, there will be the *light of heaven* to the
dying saint as he approaches that world. He has
come to the sober evening of life, but it is made
radiant by the light of that glory to which he
draws near. Bunyan gives his pilgrims, as they
approach the end of their journey, great delight in

the country of Beulah. There, as one has said,
"We seem to stand in a flood of light poured on
us from the open gates of Paradise. It falls on
every leaf and shrub by the wayside; it is reflected from the crystal streams, that between
grassy banks wind amidst groves of fruit trees into
vineyards and flower-gardens. These fields of
Beulah are just below the gate of heaven; and
with the light of heaven there come floating down
the melodies of heaven, so that here there is almost
an open revelation of the things which God hath
prepared for them that love him." They heard
voices, loud voices, from out of the City. They
met the shining ones who walked forth into this
borderland of Paradise. They had their most perfect view of the glory of the City, which was so
great that, in his utter longing for it, Christian fell
sick, sick of desire for that which was so near and
beautiful. The light of it was all around him, so
glorious that he could not, with open face, behold it. You remember the dying testimony of
one of our own eminent ministers: "The Celestial City is full in my view. Its glories have been
upon me, its breezes fan me, its odors are wafted
to me, its sounds strike upon my ears, and its
spirit is breathed into my heart. Nothing sepa-
rates me from it but the River of Death, which
now appears but as an insignificant rill, that may
be crossed at a single step, whenever God shall

give permission. The Sun of Righteousness has been gradually drawing nearer and nearer, appearing larger and brighter . . . and now he fills the whole hemisphere, pouring forth a flood of glory, in which I seem to float like an insect in the beams of the sun."

Such is the light of evening to the dying saint. We are seeing it in those who pass from us, and we shall see it as others, dear to us, come into the luminous twilight. The bells of that City of God will ring in many chambers among us. The voices of the heavenly host will sound on dying ears, as voices of great gladness. The trumpeters will be heard, saluting with ten thousand welcomes of that world, with shouting and sound of trumpet, those who are made ready to enter. There will meet them those who have harps and crowns to give unto them. And the bells of the city will ring again for joy, as they enter into the joy of their Lord. May we be of the number of such! May we walk in newness of life through the days of our trial, so that to us at evening time it shall be light.

So, too, at last, there shall be light in *the world's final evening*. To the old Crusaders there was one thing that made up for the long march and the sharp privations and the dust and smoke of roads and battle. It was the blessed city of God, the city where the Lord had lived and died.

From lands of the olive and the vine, from cities that were gaining splendor with the advancing civilization, at the call of God and the sign of the cross, they had formed themselves into vast armies, and by land and sea, in the face of all obstacles, with almost superhuman courage and strength, they had held on, until wayworn and war-scarred, they had come in sight of its renowned walls and towers, when tears of joy flowed down their bronzed faces, and there went up the shouts of armies, like the voice of thunder, " Jerusalem ! Jerusalem ! " So the ransomed of the Lord, from all these lands of earth, from all these temptations and pollutions of the world, shall return and come to Zion with songs and everlasting joy and glory on their heads; they shall obtain joy and gladness, and sorrow and sighing shall flee away. This world's long and weary day shall end in brilliant and peaceful millennium !

XVIII

THIS MINISTRY

".. I hold not my life of any account, as dear unto myself, so that I may accomplish my course, and the ministry which I received from the Lord Jesus, to testify the gospel of the grace of God."—*Acts* 20 : 24.

— ———

ON CONCLUDING AN ACTIVE PASTORATE OF THIRTY YEARS.

20

The ministry of the gospel is a bestowment from the Lord Jesus. Ministers are ambassadors accredited of Christ. Before any human call has come to them, they have been summoned into the service by a Divine Voice. Before the imposition of any human hand upon them, they have had ordination by a Divine Hand.

St. Paul wrote, "I thank him that enabled me, even Christ Jesus our Lord, for that he counted, me faithful, appointing me to his service."

So the call to preach the gospel and the appointment thereto must be from the Lord himself. They who preach the gospel have nothing to glory of; for necessity is laid upon them.

It is, therefore, a satisfaction to them when they can accomplish their course and finish the ministry which they have received from the Lord Jesus, to testify the gospel of the grace of God; and for this they would not hold their life of any account, as dear unto themselves, but rather would hold it

in willing service and sacrifice unto the end, for
Him whose they are and whom they serve.

The "dead line" in this ministry is the line of
death. It is said that some young ministers are
concerned lest the dead line will be reached when
they shall be forty years of age, lest beyond that
the churches will not want their services; and
that possibly some other vocation should be
sought by them, as that of the physician, whose
ripe experience secured by many years of practice,
makes his counsel invaluable and authoritative;
as that of the lawyer, whose many years of study
and pleading make him the authority of the bar,
and the aid of the bench.

But these alarmed incipient licentiates need a
revision of their ideas of the ministry. Woe is
unto them if they preach the gospel in fear of a
dead line, rather than in the fear of the Master;
in terror of being laid aside, rather than in joy
that the privilege is granted to them of entering
upon a course whose conclusion is determined by
another Hand!

Practice and experience are as valuable in a
clergyman as in a physician or an advocate. Care
of souls is more critical than care of bodies. The
securing of divine righteousness is on a higher
plane than the securing of human rights.

The young preacher need not discourage himself with somber images of the dead line; but he

may encourage himself with the thought of the
living issues, the immortal interests, which are
committed to his charge.

It is possible that the exactions upon the pulpit
in our day are rigid and peremptory; but the exactions upon the pulpit are greater in that which
is unexpressed than in that which is orally de-
manded. No exactions can overstate the demand
for the faithful preaching of the gospel, for the
watch for souls, for the satisfaction of Christ. In
these things lies the heaviest responsibility of the
minister.

An age of worldliness and materialism calls for
a letting down of obligation, for a reduction of the
meanings of Scripture truth, for the preaching of
smooth things, for sensationalism in the pulpit.
And there are men who court a temporary popu-
larity by feebly yielding to this call, adjourning
the eternal verities which overhang and encompass our integral life. But the real preacher de-
tects the temptation of the time, and holds fast to
the ministry of reconciliation. He has a great
work in hand for his Lord, and he cannot come
down to listen even to the clamor of a degenerate
religionism. Life is at stake! Eternity is drawing near! Unchangeable retribution awaits his
hearers!

MEN WANT TRUTH. They do not want speculation, nor fancy, nor the vanity of human judg-

ment. What saith the Lord? is the deep cry out
of the human heart. We know that things are
serious with us. We are not here for holiday.
A laugh answers no great question. A supposi-
tion has no quality of revelation. The discussion
of worldly relations cannot settle future destiny.

What shall I do to be saved? is the overmas-
tering inquiry that crowds out all others. It is
the preacher's task to answer that to each soul; to
the thoughtful and to the careless as well. For,
sooner or later, each one becomes an inquirer.
Some may not become so till it is late, perhaps
too late. But all want the answer; they want to
be familiar with it, so familiar that they can retain
it, that they can recall it in storm, in shipwreck,
at midnight, in the wild whirl of flood, in the roar
of battle, in the crash of doom, wherever men
die.

The gospel, the glad word, the blessed evangel,
must be fastened in the mind of every hearer,
must be wrought in illuminated words upon the
memory, so that if the sinner be alone in his supreme moment, with no mother by him, no friend
to speak to him, no minister to pray for him, he
shall yet remember the divine message, and know
that the forgiving Christ is ready to respond to
his faith!

This truth holds satisfaction in it. It has been
proved. That Christ died to save sinners has met

the need of men everywhere. Salvation by the blood of the Redeemer sounds on imperiled souls with a gospel tone. Lower terms, other teachings, weak surmises, only tantalize those who hunger and thirst for the Bread of Life and the Water of Life, who want *certainly to know how they can be saved now*. They will not thank you, in the decisive crises of life, for your invented doctrine, for your vain cry of peace, for your untempered mortar. They want something to build on that will stand: something firmer than your unsifted sand; and nothing less than the real Word of God, the tried and sound Word, will avail. Show us the way of life and lead us therein! is the demand on the preacher of this day, and of all days. Give us the very truth that our poor, sinful souls are yearning for; and give it simply and earnestly, and as though you meant what you are saying. Give us doctrine that will stand the test of the judgment day: such that you can look into our faces at the tribunal of God!

But there be teachers who say, The times have changed: truth is evolvent: we are learning some things that the fathers did not know: theology is a progressive science and new meanings are found for the old doctrines.

Undoubtedly new light shines out of the Word. It shines *to make the old truths clearer*, and not to obscure them or blot them out. Sin is the same

fact now that it always has been. Salvation by
the redemption of Christ is as certain a doctrine
to me as it was to St. Paul. Justification by faith
in Christ is as clearly a truth for a sinner to-day
as it was for Luther when it flashed into his mind,
as, on his knees, he was wearily climbing Peter's
staircase at Rome. We need to know, and to
have it impressed upon us, as much as men ever
needed it, that we are finally to be judged by the
deeds done here in the body and that our eternal
happiness or our eternal misery are to have decision now. We should recognize the central fact
that Christ was the true Light which lighteth
every man coming into the world: and that those
who are not saved by him in the existent probation are without excuse.

Now, whatever scientific research may unfold,
or philosophic reasoning may conclude, these old
truths cannot be changed. They are fundamental. They are immutable. They are granitic: and
they give substance and strength and enduring-
ness and reliability to true theology.

Times may change and men may change with
them: other forms of truth may have revision:
but these substantive doctrines abide the same
from age to age. Like the fixed stars, they shine
with the same light and from the same heaven
through the enduring centuries.

The minister is a teacher of divine truth. He

is a man of One Book. He speaks under inspired orders. " Preach unto it the preaching that I bid thee" is his charge. He speaks to the intellect of men ; to their sober reason and their unperverted conscience. He has the best part of every man with him. He speaks to the sensibilities ; to human hopes and fears, to the longing of souls that have telescopic vision and look into the distances of the eternal years. He speaks to the will ; and presents motives of force and of supreme importance to sway it to right choice. He speaks of themes that are sacred, that live in the holy memories of childhood, that reverberate with the murmur of mother voices, that have been wrought into the structure of his whole lifetime, and that wear the crown of a rightful supremacy.

The destructive criticism of our day is doing dangerous work. It is doing work which will need to be undone. It is undermining faith in the most important truths. Professedly eliminating error, it is really sowing the seeds of vaster error. It is fostering unfaith in place of the most sacred and vital of all beliefs. Its effect on the popular mind is unsettling and ruinous. It creates a pervasive atmosphere of doubt. It antagonizes preaching and teaching and all efforts for success and power in the saving of souls. It displaces the Bible from the thought and reverence and controlling authority of men. They are as navigators at sea without reckoning or compass or chart.

Just here we must be on guard. Just here the pulpit must reassert itself. Just at this point we must raise again the old war-cry of the Reformation: The Bible! The Bible alone! Now for the truth and for the imperiled cause, we must demand INVIOLABLENESS FOR THE WORD OF GOD. By that we stand or fall. By that, in the name of Him who gave it, we set up our unretreating banners.

The Spirit is in the Word. He effectually uses the Word. These words are words which the Spirit teacheth. St. Paul thanked God that the Thessalonian Christians accepted "the word of the message, even the word of God, . . . not as the word of men, but, as it is in truth, the word of God, which also worketh in you that believe." He wrote to the Romans that belief cometh of hearing, and hearing by the Word of Christ. He charged the Ephesians, "take . . . the sword of the Spirit, which is the word of God." He put at the forefront of his letter to the Hebrews, " God, having of old time spoken unto the fathers in the prophets by divers portions and in divers manners." He wrote to his beloved child Timothy, " Thou hast known the sacred writings which are able to make thee wise unto salvation through faith, which is in Christ Jesus." We plant ourselves, at this crisis, on the reiterated testimony of our Lord Himself: " Ye search the scriptures, and these are they which bear witness of me : " . . . and upon his later word, " The scripture cannot be broken :" and upon his tender prayer, " Sanctify them in the truth : thy word is truth."

Here we stand. No adverse criticism can move us. With our fathers we rest on the imperishable Word. With the saints of all ages we exalt the inspired Word of the Lord. We know what it has done for us. We know what a power of grace and salvation, of enlightenment, of liberty, of education, it has been in all our history. We owe our freedom, our culture, our rank among nations, to the Bible. It was a significant act when the queen of England, in reply to the question of a barbaric prince, what it is that has made her empire great, put into his hands a copy of the Holy Scriptures. Its fruits maintain the Word. If there were no internal evidence of its divinity, the external evidence would be enough. We forswear our manhood, our civilization, our victorious progress in the world, when we decline to give the Bible its sole place of authority. We reject salvation, our hopes of heaven, the whole work of our redeeming Christ, when we reject the revelation of Holy Scripture.

The minister sets forth also the ethics of practical every-day life, the rules of right action in

homes, in business, in politics, in all the affairs of
the people. He teaches that human conduct
should be squared by the Golden Rule. His influence is an educational influence: it leads to
right development; refining, upbuilding, broadening the popular tastes and choices. You may
trace the instruction of the pulpit through any
community where it has been a factor for molding
the life, in the morals, the schools and homes of
the people. It urges to that which is higher: at
last to that which is highest.

We hear much of the sphere of the pulpit: its
claims and power are set in contrast with other
spheres. But after all is said, this remains: that
the work of the pulpit is evermore with immutable
verities of life and of eternity. It defines the responsibilities of free agency: warns men against
the temptations that beguile them into evil: declares the sinfulness of sin: holds up the standard
of duty, God's moral law: makes the one way of
redemption plain: draws men to noblest life and
to heavenly aspirations. Surely this is sphere
enough. St. Paul, with all his culture and power,
thought it was enough for him to testify to men,
at Athens, at Rome, in voluptuous Corinth or
barbarian Melita, the gospel of the grace of God:
not law, not morality, not speculation, not human
conclusions, but the gospel of the grace of God!
In the preaching of that is power and wisdom

and success and the favor of God and the co-working of the Spirit, and so salvation and eternal glory!

While the pulpit has been called the "preacher's throne" and while his greatest effort should be put forth in what St. Paul called "preaching the kingdom," the minister has an important work to do as the pastor of his flock. Some ministers have made it a point to know all their people by name, even the youngest of the children. Certainly the pastor who would exert the deepest influence would seek to know the spiritual condition of every individual in his parish. This knowledge would be invaluable, not only as guiding his efforts for their personal salvation, but also as suggesting the themes and the substance of his public discourse.

It is told of Robert Hall that in his parochial visits he liked to steal in earlier than he was expected that he might for a time share in the gambols and gaieties of the children. The pastor's acquaintance should begin early with the children. If he remains long in one place, they will soon be the young people of his charge and then at the head of their own homes. So rapidly do the generations pass across the stage!

The conditions of human life, the trials which come to all households, make a strong claim upon the sympathies of the affectionate pastor. He enters into their experiences, rejoices in their joy, sorrows in their sadness, is glad to supplement their feebleness and fear by his courage and strength and faith. They naturally appeal to him for spiritual counsel, seek his guidance in the stress of storm and trouble, ask his benediction as they go out into untried paths and take upon their shoulders unusual burdens, listen to his voice when the sense of sin makes them feel the need of a Saviour, look to him for prayer in their behalf when the waves and billows of calamity and death pour over them.

And it is the joy of the pastor that in Christ's stead he can be the minister of help and consolation and hope to those for whom he watches as the shepherd for the flock.

The ultimate success of the minister's labors is closely allied to his pastoral work. Impressions which are produced by preaching are transient unless they can be followed by personal influence. That which is spoken in the pulpit is spoken to the great congregation: but the word that is said when eye looks into eye and when the touch of the hand is felt, is the word that means the individual, as when Nathan said to David, " Thou art the man." The pastor must imitate the divine Shepherd who said, " I know mine own and mine own know me." All that interests them is of interest to him. He is concerned for their mate-

rial welfare, for their moral interests, for their
spiritual good.

The great events, the supreme crises of life, are
constantly occurring somewhere, in some homes,
in some souls of a large parish. The minister is
needed then: and he goes with words of cheer
and solace and life to his glad or sorrowing or
fearful people.

This parish has always expected, it has always
needed, much pastoral work. Requiring, for the
last sixteen years, of its minister but one preaching
service on each Sabbath day, it has had more of
private and personal work than is common, and
the church has prospered with this arrangement.
It is this personal work which has exacted
strength and time, and which has also secured, by
the divine blessing, precious results. Any church,
certainly this church, cannot prosper without the
house to house, hand to hand, soul to soul, labor
of a diligent and loving pastor. At the same time,
the period is now reached when the interests of
the parish, when its self-protection as well, require
a Sunday evening preaching service.

The ministry which is to be finished here to-
day has been a long one as pastorates are in these
times. It has not been an an over-long one measured by the standard of former days.

Thirty years in this age of restlessness and
change, when the demand for novelty and sensa-

tionalism is strong and perverse, is quite an
extended period for one man to hold the attention
and the affection of one parish.

If, in speaking of this period, I shall transgress
my own rule by bringing forward that which is
personal and statistical to some extent, I shall be
pardoned in view of the peculiarity of the occasion
and your expressed desire.

I lay down my office to-day, as, twenty-nine
years ago in the same place and for the same reason, I laid it down, because I have not strength of
voice for all the work which this large church requires. A weakness of the vocal organs, first in-
duced by over-labor when a young man for this
people, in a time of wide and powerful religious
interest, when more than two hundred souls were
led to Christ, and when I felt that the life would
be long which answered life's great end, and that
the saving of the souls of this flock would more
than compensate for any disability which might
come to the shepherd of it, has once before interrupted my work, as it is now interfering with it
again.

I have never been a candidate; and so do not know
the peculiar pleasure of standing before a critical
audience in that relation. It was in the middle of
my senior year as a student of theology that I
received the unanimous call of this church and
society to become their pastor. Seven months

after that, on the first day of October, nearly forty-three years ago, I received ordination to the ministry here. For fourteen years I served this church; then was absent for nearly thirteen years; and now finish sixteen years of renewed service. Although quite a number of invitations have come to me, from six different states of the Union and from foreign fields to places of labor with what might be considered superior attractions, I have been content to dwell among mine own people and to labor with them year after year for the cause which has here been committed to us.

It would be difficult to detach from the memories of the generation and a half which now pass as in panorama before us all those things which were full of significance and interest at their occurrence. It will be enough to indicate a few salient features of the pastorate.

It is gratefully recalled that these years of our life together have been a period of unbroken harmony. Whatever differences of sentiment and taste there may have been, they have subsided before the supreme purpose of loyalty to Christ and his Church. We have gone on as a Brotherhood under the control of our great Leader, and to-day we can remember only the things in which we have been agreed. We might challenge the finding of another such relation which in this respect has been more blessed.

21

These years hold a long record of kindnesses
which began at their beginning and have continued to their end; out of which stand forth my
release for two prolonged absences in Europe
and another at the West and the joyous celebra-
tion of my silver wedding anniversary.

In them are hallowed seasons of deep religious
interest, when the truth has taken strong hold of
the people, and many have been won to Christ;
resulting, at the close of 1848 and the beginning of
1849 in the addition of one hundred and twenty-
four persons to the fellowship of the church; in
October, 1858, in the addition of twenty-six; in
May and July, 1877, of sixty-six; in May, 1883,
of thirty-four; and of smaller numbers at many
communion seasons.

Many sad and tender occasions have gathered
us in sympathy with those who have mourned
for the loss of the fairest and best beloved; children in their beauty; friends in the opulence of
their love, and when their presence and help were
most desired. So, too, have we met in common
joy, when marriage-bells were ringing, and when
glad voices wakened responsive music in our
hearts.

Names spring to-day to our thought, if not to
our lips, so many, of the beloved, " dear, near and
true," who stood with us, sharers of our burdens,
sharers, too, of the joy in accomplishment, ever

faithful, firm in the tests of friendship, cheering us by their unwavering confidence and courage; some of them already privileged and crowned and awaiting us with Christ, for where he is there are they with him; some still in the service, witnessing for the Master to whom they have given their lives.

This time of retrospection is also a time of anticipation. We would not forget, we cannot forget, those with whom we took sweet counsel and in whose company we walked to the house of God. We look on, also, to the day when we all, those who have gone before us, and we who have lingered a little longer at our tasks, shall be gathered in the place which Christ has prepared for us, when he whom we dearly love shall be our Shepherd, and shall guide us unto fountains of waters of life. We anticipate the greeting which awaits us from those who have been already honored, and who have become used to the scenes and service which are for all the redeemed.

Great changes, during the period at which we are hastily glancing, have occurred in every direction, in all the relations of human society. All the clergy who were members of the council for my ordination, with two exceptions, are dead. There is no pastor remaining in the county who was a pastor then. There is but one minister beside myself in the whole state who was then the minister of the church of which he is now the minister. Of the members of the church and society at that time very few remain with us. Then, there were in these Quinnipiack wards three churches; now, there are eight churches; two chapels, one built by a member of this church, are also occupied on the outskirts of the parish, making ten meeting-houses instead of three. This was the only Congregational church, now there are three. Then, there was hardly a dwelling west of this spot; since that, from the banks of the Quinnipiack population has spread up the hillsides eastward, and over the plain westward. Then, there were two small schoolhouses; now, the Woolsey district has its stately buildings and its splendid appointments for public school instruction, with thirty-two trained teachers.

The four hundred and forty-two funerals which I have attended, and the marriage of four hundred and sixty-six persons which I have solemnized indicate in part the mutations of the rolling years.

Our location, in itself most beautiful, on this commanding and tranquil site, properly, as that of the old First Church, in front of the ground whose silent dwellers make an ever-growing census, and looking out over the enlarging populations of the living, is yet one which subjects us to necessary reverses. A suburban church feels the flow of life, backward and forward, into the heart of the old city, and out into the freedom of the country. So we have dismissed a large number of members to the city churches west of us, and have parted with a large colony, numbering in the end between one hundred and two hundred, for the building of our sister church east of us. The new Ferry Street Church has also drawn upon our membership. Drafts are constantly made upon the mother-church of any community; younger churches feel the need of help and increase; and we have borne the effects of their enlargement.

During the last decade we have seen great inroads upon our strength by death. Two beloved and honored office-bearers, men of might, with an unusual number of citizens of personal and financial weight, have been removed from us, whose loss has been heavily felt in all our Christian activities.

The entire roll of the church, from the beginning in 1830, has one thousand, three hundred and seventy-seven names. Of these, seventy-eight constituted the church at and near its organization. During the four pastorates other than mine, three hundred and ninety-nine persons were received to membership, an average of one hundred to each pastorate, and a yearly average of sixteen. In the earlier period of fourteen years of my service, three hundred and four persons; in the latter period of sixteen years, five hundred and ninety-

one persons have been added to your fellowship;
in all, eight hundred and ninety-five communi-
cants, five hundred and fifty-four of these on confession of faith, making an annual average addition
of thirty members. The increase of the church
during the thirty years we are now reviewing, as
well as the yearly average of increase, has been
about twice as much as during the twenty-nine
years beside.

During the six months of this year, 1889, twen-
ty-four have been added to our membership, a
considerably larger number than the average;
fourteen of them at the last observance of the
Holy Communion, making the occasion one of
most glad and tender interest.

I have administered baptism to three hundred
and seventy-three persons, an average of more
than twelve each year.

There is satisfaction, also, in our external progress and improvements. It has been my delight
to help you in that advance which has taken us
out of what is now the Grand Avenue school-
house, and which led early to the erection of a
chapel which marked an era of new life; after
seven years to the securing of this site, and the
erection and furnishing of this commodious house;
in 1880 to the enlargement of this building, which
has given us the spacious Sunday-school room,
the chapel, and our social rooms; then to the

purchase of a new bell to take the place of a
similar one which was broken, and to the enlarged
compass and improvement of the organ; and
later to the renovation and refurnishing of the
entire house of worship; all of which has been
accomplished during the years we are now con-
sidering.

The church has now on its roll five hundred
and three names: quite a number of them, notwithstanding our effort to have absentees take
letters of dismission, being permanently away.

The succession of orthodox pastors, men holding the great essential doctrines of the Word of
God and preaching them plainly and with power,
by which this church has been favored from the
first, has given the truth firm foothold in this community, and has resulted in revivals of religion
which have developed sound Christian character.

The power of the church here has been an uplifting and saving power, which should be increas-
ingly set forth. There is ability, unemployed or
half employed, to secure still greater results in all
our work: latent strength sufficient to move
society from its foundations: professional and
business capacity, broad intelligence and experience, waiting for attention to the Master's call for
service: pecuniary strength ample to secure a
high order of talent in the services of public wor-

ship, in the offices of praise and the preaching of the Word.

The minister, for the greatest efficiency of his ministry, needs a church not only fully equipped, but also fully employed. Dr. Parkhurst has lately said, "The preacher's church is his force, not his field." The whole church should be with him. Rev. John McNeill, who has lately come down from Scotland to London, has said to his London audience, "I am not going to spend my strength in preaching only on churchgoers." The unconverted who come to church are no more important than the unconverted who do not come. The force of the church should cover the wider field.

Still the testifying of the gospel of the grace of God sounds on in its winning tones. The blessed Saviour does not despair of gaining the hearts that have been shut, oh, so long! to his tender call. For you he has stood, looking in at your windows, knocking at your doors, saying, Open to me! till his head is filled with dew and his locks with the drops of the night. And to-day he calls again. He would not have you lost. The hands that he reaches out to you are wounded hands, wounded for you! Might it be that in this serious evening of years the voice that has spoken to you so often for him might even now awaken response and be answered back by the cry of faith?

Dr. Johnson is quoted as saying, " No one ever

did *anything* consciously for the last time without a feeling of sadness." Our best work is imperfect work. As we look back upon it we see its defects and wonder whether if we had been more faithful greater results might have been seen. So I wonder to-day whether anything I might have done or said would have made this a stronger church: would have made these who profess to follow Christ more like the Master: would have brought the impenitent to accept the salvation the gospel offers; and then a strain of sadness runs into the harmonies of the time.

Still the joy remains that the service has been done, the honest attempt has been made, the burden of the Lord has been borne. The joy is not, as a friend has said to me, that the burden is now to be laid down, but that it has been borne: not that there is to be a riddance of the burden, but that into the life and being, into the character and the eternal life has gone the grandeur of having borne the burden. The burden is not a load to be cast off, it is not something that has crushed one, but something that has lifted one, and it is laid down as a means of ascent to something higher, as men lay down solid stepping-stones on which they rise into holy temples and structures of imperishable glory!

And now, after all these years, with their manifold experiences, after the joy of forming friendships which have been begun here and which are to remain eternal, after service which has been done for the beloved Master and which has brought satisfaction to him in the souls that are saved, it is indeed a relief to find that our ways are not to diverge from this point to unite no more in this world, but that, through your consideration and kindness in offering me the place and title of PASTOR EMERITUS, which I now accept in the genuine spirit of confidence with which it was cheerfully given, our fellowship is to be continued and so there is no necessity of parting nor of saying the sad word, Farewell.

And now, my friends, I commend you to God, and to the word of his grace, which is able to build you up, and to give you the inheritance among all them that are sanctified. And the peace of God, which passeth all understanding, shall guard your hearts and your thoughts in Christ Jesus. The grace of the Lord Jesus Christ be with you. Amen.

www.ingramcontent.com/pod-product-compliance
Lightning Source LLC
Chambersburg PA
CBHW021124270326
41929CB00009B/1041